# Saint Katharine Drexel

## Pioneer for Human Rights

**Daniel McSheffery**

**Resurrection Press**
An Imprint of
**Catholic Book Publishing Co.**
Totowa · New Jersey

All direct quotations are from the Archives of the Sisters of the Blessed Sacrament (1892-1955).

Grateful acknowledgement is made to Stephanie Morris, Ph.D., Director of Archives and Sister M. Ruth Spain, S.B.S., Director of the St. Katharine Guild.

First published in March 2002 by
　　　　　　　　Catholic Book Publishing/Resurrection Press
　　　　　　　　77 West End Road
　　　　　　　　Totowa, NJ 07512

ISBN 1-878718-71-1
Library of Congress Catalog Card Number: 2001-135975

Cover design by John Murello
Cover and inside photos by Sister M. Ruth Catherine Spain, S.B.S.

Printed in Canada

*To my sisters*

*Kathleen Doll*

*and*

*Ann Andrus*

# Acknowledgements

I would like to thank the Sisters of the Blessed Sacrament
for all their cooperation.
A special word of gratitude to those who helped
with the research: Melayna and Bill Lovelace,
MaryKathryn Hart, Lorraine Fiore and
Margaret Kiernan.

# Contents

# Introduction

## DEFINING MOMENTS

Throughout the history of the Church many of our great saints had defining moments in their lives. As a result of the words of someone else they made important decisions that dramatically changed the course of their lives and directed them along the road to greater sanctity. They heard a voice and responded to a God-given vocation that had a profound effect on their lives and the lives of those who came to know and love them.

It happened in the town of Nazareth when the angel Gabriel appeared to a young virgin who was engaged to be married. And the angel said to her, "You shall conceive and bear a son and give him the name Jesus. He will be called the Son of the Most High." Mary accepted this vocation with the words, "Let it be done to me as you say." By accepting that vocation her life and the course of history was changed.

A few years after the resurrection of the Lord, Saul was on the road to the city of Damascus to arrest those who had accepted the Christian faith. With a flash of light he suddenly fell to the ground and heard a voice say, "I am Jesus, the one you are persecuting." Saul the persecutor became Paul the Apostle who accepted the vocation of preaching to the Gentiles.

In the year 387 the great philosopher Augustine found himself attracted to Christianity. As he meditated in the garden in the city of Milan he heard a school girl singing, *"Tolle lege, tolle lege."* ("Pick up and read.") Responding he picked up the scripture, opened to a passage, read, and came to accept the Christian faith and become one of the Church's greatest bishops and saints.

It was in the year 1887 that Katharine Drexel, a young heiress from Philadelphia, while on a European vacation, experienced a similar defining moment. She had suddenly lost her father and was in poor health. To help her recuperate from the illness, her two sisters accompanied her on a trip to Europe.

The wealthy heiress had developed a concern for the plight of blacks and Native Americans in the ghettos and reservations in her native land. A family friend, Bishop James O'Connor of Omaha, had established an order of sisters to work in his missionary diocese but there were no priests available for service. He asked Katharine to try to find an order of priests who would be willing to come to his mission fields. In response, she asked for help from several monasteries throughout Europe without any success.

Although she was concerned about the missionary work among blacks and Native Americans, Katharine felt that she was being called to join a group of contemplative nuns and visited several convents during her journey.

The three young, unmarried sisters were excited to learn that the bishop had arranged for them a private audience with the Holy Father Pope Leo XIII. They spent a great deal of time talking about what they would have to say to him and what they would ask him. The audience quickly became the highlight of what had been an exciting and enjoyable European vacation. They spent the night before in animated conversation about how they were to dress and act at the audience. On the morning of January 27 they were taken into the throne room of the apostolic palace to meet with the spiritual leader of their beloved Church.

Throughout the entire European tour Katharine kept a daily diary which provided a complete record of what happened at each stop on their vacation travels. The diaries are still intact in the archives at the motherhouse of the Sisters of the Blessed Sacrament.

Katharine described what happened at that defining moment of her young life. In her diary we read, "Then we went to Rome and had a private audience with Pope Leo XIII. Kneeling at his feet, my girlish fancy thought that surely God's Vicar would not refuse me. So I pleaded for missionary priests for Bishop O'Connor's Indians. To my astonishment His Holiness responded, 'Why not, my child, yourself become a missionary?' In reply I said, 'Because, Holy Father, sisters can be had for the missions, but no priests.'"

The diary account of the audience ends here abruptly. Nothing more was said about her request. Apparently, the Holy Father made no further attempt to persuade her. It was not until many years later that she told her sisters that once she left the palace she could not get away from the Vatican fast enough. Once outside she sobbed and sobbed. She was initially frightened at the implications of the pope's words. Gradually, after much prayerful meditation and the help of her spiritual director, she accepted the advice of the Holy Father and gave up the idea of a contemplative vocation. She founded a new religious order and spent her life and her considerable fortune championing the cause of black and Native Americans who were forced to live a life of poverty and discrimination.

Her defining moment opened a new era of justice and freedom for untold numbers of her fellow Americans whose lives were touched by St. Katharine Drexel and the Sisters of the Blessed Sacrament she founded. Pope Leo XIII's question and the young heiress's answer had a profound effect on the cause of Catholic social justice during the 20th century.

# CHAPTER 1

# THE BEGINNINGS

It had been a difficult pregnancy. The birth and the hours that followed were even more difficult for mother, child, doctor, father and other family members. It was on the cold and gray morning of November 26 in 1858 at the Drexel home on Race Street in a fashionable section of the city of Philadelphia. The birth resulted in a serious cause for concern for the welfare of mother and baby, and for most of the morning both their lives hung in the balance. It was noon before the mother Hannah Jane seemed out of danger, but the Drexel family doctor had serious doubts about the baby's ability to survive the ordeal.

After talking over the situation with the child's father, Francis Anthony Drexel, the doctor urged the young man to go up to the bedroom and reassure his wife that everything possible would be done for the child. With fear in her eyes she said, "Anthony, tell me she is going to be all right." Looking into her eyes, filled with fear, he tried to reassure her as best he could by saying, "Our daughter will be fine in a couple of days."

Quickly the young couple decided to name the new born daughter after her paternal grandmother Katharine Drexel. Still apprehensive about the health of his daughter, Francis decided that he could not wait until the arrangements could be made for a traditional church baptism. As soon as his wife closed her eyes in sleep, he took a glass of water and poured a few drops on the forehead of his child and baptized her in the name of the Holy Trinity, and so it came about that Katharine Mary became a Christian on the day of her birth. Almost from that moment her health began to improve and soon her three-year-old sister Elizabeth and other members of the family were happily visiting the Drexel's second born daughter.

The young mother was less fortunate. Soon after the birth of her second child, her strength seemed to falter. She was weak for the first few days after childbirth and about a week later she developed a fever and within another week she became delirious. Francis, the busy banker, abandoned the office to stay at his wife's bedside and try to make her more comfortable. Daily her condition worsened.

A few days before Christmas her doctors gave up hope for her recovery. The only consolation to the family was that in her mostly unconscious state she felt no real pain. The holidays were a difficult occasion for all. Seeking to help in any way they could, Francis' younger brother Anthony and his new wife Ellen took Elizabeth to their Philadelphia home in an effort to make the holiday season as pleasant as possible for her.

Christmas day and night the distraught husband kept a lonely vigil spending much of the time placing cool compresses on her forehead and kneeling at her side in prayer. On December 28 it began to seem as though the miracle he sought would be granted. Late in the afternoon the fever lessened and she regained consciousness. Still unable to speak with her family, she smiled when she was told that the formal baptism of her baby would take place the next day.

The Church of the Assumption was still aglow with Christmas decorations when the Drexel family presented their child for the ceremonies. Her godmother and aunt, Mary Drexel Lankenau, proudly held Katharine in her arms as the newborn officially became a member of the Roman Catholic Church. Following the ceremony the family hurried home so that Hannah Jane might share their joy. The proud father brought the baby to her mother's bedside. His wife managed to smile to the delight of all those who had come to celebrate.

Following a brief and subdued celebration the family left and Francis resumed his vigil at the bedside of his stricken wife. Before his eyes she seemed to be slipping back into unconsciousness. The doctor was quickly called. He told her husband that her condition had quickly worsened. He then added the words no one wanted to hear, "There is no hope for her recovery."

As morning dawned the day after her daughter's baptism, Hannah Jane breathed her last. She was buried in the Quaker churchyard of the Langstroch family in Germantown, Pennsylvania. Years later when retired and preparing for her own death, Mother Katharine Drexel had her mother's body reburied in the Drexel family crypt. She had gotten permission for the reburial of her Baptist Quaker mother after the chancery office found evidence that Hannah Jane had expressed a desire to become a Catholic some months before her death.

Throughout her life, the grateful daughter who had never had the opportunity to know and love her mother in life, showed her devotion and gratitude by seeing to it that she should find a resting place along with the other members of her family. She was always deeply grateful to the woman who gave her life and lost her own life in the process. She never forgot and never ceased to pray for her and honor her memory.

In the weeks following the death of his wife, Francis felt that he could not adequately take care of his two young girls and provide them a proper home. When he returned to his now lonely home, he felt that Elizabeth and Katharine needed a mother's care in their earliest years. His brother Anthony and his wife Ellen came forward and offered to take the children. Their brief period of babysitting during the holiday season had convinced them that they could live up to the additional responsibility of caring for their young nieces. Their father was very grateful for he knew that Ellen would make a delightful foster mother and provide his young ones with the love and affection they needed.

With the help of other loving members of the family, the two children spent the next fourteen months in the care of their relatives. Their temporary parents provided for their every need and a bond of love was forged that would last throughout their lives. They were extremely family oriented and in the time of need they generously lavished affection on the youngsters placed in their charge.

It was in April of 1860 that Francis told his children that they would be coming home to live with him and his soon-to-be new wife Emma Bouvier. The children were thrilled. The wedding was one of the grandest ever held in the city. The ceremony was held at beautifully decorated Old St. Joseph Church accompanied by a full orchestra and special choir. The local newspapers described every detail of the elaborate celebration. Following the ceremony the young couple left for what the newspapers reported would be "a short European tour."

Actually the short tour lasted six months and included most of the important cities of Europe and featured a private audience with Pope Pius IX. It was mid October when they returned to their new home in a most fashionable section of their native city. Their home on Walnut Street offered the new family all of the luxuries that a wealthy banker could provide. Their beautifully furnished home contained all of the amenities of the finest homes in the city.

The deep religious faith of the young couple played an important role in the furnishing of their fashionable home. The new Mrs. Drexel was a devoted Catholic who personally supervised the construction of a special oratory. Here she and her family gathered for daily prayer. It was furnished with a beautiful altar, crucifix and paintings. A special feature was an impressive statue of the Blessed Virgin Mary on a large corner pedestal. The moments the family spent in their prayer room had a profound effect on the lives of the Drexel children.

In addition to their impressive home in the city, each summer Francis rented a house in the country. This provided the children with acres of farmland in which they could spend the carefree summer hours. The happy family enjoyed the wonders of nature on their private estate. Each evening mother and children would hurry down to the railroad station to meet Francis after a busy day in the bank in Philadelphia. Many a delightful evening they spent in the rustic retreat listening to the young mother telling her children about the lives of their favorite saints.

In the summer of 1863 tragedy struck the Drexel family. It was in the middle of the Civil War and the banking firm experienced tremendous growth. So great was the volume of business that the founder Francis Martin Drexel, who had retired, was called back to the firm. On June 6 while returning from a business trip to Pottstown, he slipped and fell while getting off the train. He died the next day as a result of his injuries. It was a serious loss for his wife, his sons and his grandchildren who greatly revered him.

The next important date in their young lives was October 2, 1863. On this day, Louise was born and her young sisters enthusiastically welcomed her into their family. From the very beginning until the day she died Katharine referred to her as "my little sister." Their loving mother always treated all three of them as her children without any distinction. She showered on all three of the girls the same love and affection. Frequently Francis spoke of how fortunate he was to have found a new wife who was such a perfect mother for his beloved children. The five Drexels were bound together with a bond of love that grew stronger throughout the happy years of their childhood on Walnut Street.

Emma Bouvier Drexel was in many ways a remarkable woman. She came from a family of wealth and prominence in the community. She was well educated and at ease with the leading women in Philadelphia society. As a result, she was frequently invited to social affairs of all kinds. Though she seemed to enjoy these gatherings, she set aside time to help meet the needs of the city's poorer families. She was generous with her time and her great financial resources.

Shortly after she established the family home on Walnut Street, she began the practice of opening the doors to all people of need regardless of their nationality or religious affiliation. In her well known history, *The Francis A. Drexel Family*, Sister Dolores Letterhouse wrote about the open house that Emma conducted at her home. Each week, usually on Mondays, Wednesdays and Thursdays, she welcomed all who sought her help. She provided counseling and someone to talk to. She set aside a large sum of money to help with the payment of rent and the purchase of food and clothing. Each week she spent hours speaking to those who would have no knowledgeable person to talk with. Her home became a well known refuge for the socially downtrodden in the teeming city.

As the girls grew older, they were encouraged to follow the example of their mother. In later years, Katharine would put into practice many of the methods her mother used to meet the needs of as many as possible during these busy afternoons.

To operate in a more efficient manner, a social worker was hired by the family to help determine those who were in the greatest need. As the program grew, Emma set aside more than $20,000 a year to distribute among those who came for help. In the religious life, Katharine adopted many of her mother's methods as she reached out to help in the Native American and black missions she established.

It was during these early years that Emma's mother decided that her daughter needed some assistance in raising three young girls with a pious Catholic upbringing. She made what proved to be a fantastic choice. She had working for her a young woman who was forced to leave the convent because of her frail constitution. Johanna Ryan would prove to be an invaluable nanny and a confidant and friend for the young girls. She came and stayed for the rest of her life. Her influence on the children was an important factor in their spiritual growth and their commitment to service.

Johanna continued to live the life of a religious in her new home. Her piety and her life of prayer gave a shining example of Christian living to the young girls in her charge. They loved, respected and imitated her. When out of their parents' earshot, they sometimes referred to her as "Father Ryan." She was strict with them and in a special way encouraged Katharine to consider a religious vocation.

Katharine grew up to know and love three grandmothers. Elizabeth Langstroth, the mother of Hannah Drexel, was a strict Quaker who sought to encourage her girl grandchildren to learn how to live as simple housewives. She carefully taught them to crochet, to keep a tidy house and to prepare nourishing meals for their men folk. She spoke with great formality and was very upset when her grandchildren did not use their full Christian names. When they came to visit her she insisted they refer to each other as Elizabeth and Katharine and on numerous occasions told them that, "Lizzie is a hideous name and Kate is too short."

Each week Emma took her three small girls to visit her mother Louise Bouvier, a dignified, formal and elegantly dressed lady. She was respected by a large family who looked upon her as a matriarch. Emma had ten brothers and sisters. The most famous of her family was her brother John's great granddaughter, Jacqueline Bouvier Kennedy. The young girls enjoyed their visits with their grandparents, aunts and uncles.

Katharine developed a special relationship with her paternal grandmother, Catherine Drexel, who after her husband's death continued to live in the old family homestead. The girls cherished the afternoons they spent with her and they especially enjoyed the home-made cookies she always baked for them. Grandmother Drexel had a great influence on the girls until the time of her death when Katharine was twelve years old.

The first years of her education Katie spent at her mother's knee. Here she learned her prayers and developed a devotion to the Blessed Virgin Mary that became a great part of her religious life. While her older sister attended convent school down the road from their Walnut Street home, she took her lessons in the familiar atmosphere of the family home. From the very beginning she loved to write and the collection in the archives of the Blessed Sacrament Sisters tells us much about these early days.

One of her memorable experiences occurred when she was nine years old and her mother took her to Lizzie's First Communion celebration in the convent chapel. She was very impressed with the ceremony and began to long for the day she would receive the Eucharistic Lord. Katie loved a party and was delighted to be invited to a lavish breakfast that her mother gave for members of the class. She had such a wonderful time that she asked her mother to promise that she would have a breakfast on her great day.

Her aunt Madame Louise Bouvier, a Religious of the Sacred Heart, prepared her for First Communion Day. Sister Louise was upset because her young niece seemed more concerned about the breakfast than the church ceremony. Shortly before the day she wrote of her concern in a letter. She wrote, "Why do you speak so much of the breakfast and say so little about the thoughts and feelings that possess you at that great moment you receive Our Lord for the first time?"

When the great day came Katie came to appreciate both parts of the celebration and throughout her whole life the Eucharist played a central role. But like many of her friends she delighted in the pretty clothes she wore and asked her mother to "Put lots of lace and ruffles on my things."

On June 3, 1870, Philadelphia Archbishop John F. Wood celebrated the First Communion Mass. The young people were impressed when he told them that this was the most important day in their lives, but that every time they received Communion they should do so with the same devotion and love. According to the custom of the day, the archbishop also administered the Sacrament of Confirmation to the eleven-year-old children.

Katharine did not communicate to her aunt and other relatives the devotion she felt on that day. As was her custom, she was a private person and did not often speak about her religious devotions. It was in fact fifty years after that First Communion Day that she made her feelings known in some retreat notes that she wrote in 1920. According to the Archives of the Sisters of the Blessed Sacrament, she described her feelings in these words: "I remember my First Communion. Jesus made me shed my tears because of his greatness in stooping and coming to me, mite that I was."

She rarely spoke to others, even her own sisters, of her genuine love and devotion to the Eucharistic Lord. So often in her life, her actions spoke much louder than her words.

# CHAPTER 2

# THE DREXEL FAMILY SCHOOL

Mary Ann Cassidy was the principal. She had an outstanding faculty including Francis and Emma Drexel. She had a beautifully furnished classroom with all of the latest equipment—comfortable chairs and desks, modern blackboards, wall maps and the best writing utensils. All of these facilities were to help provide a good Catholic education to a student body that numbered three—Elizabeth, Katharine and Louise Drexel. This unique school was located in a large room located in the Drexel mansion on Walnut Street in Philadelphia.

Miss Cassidy, as she was known by the family and her fellow teachers, came to supervise the education of the girls at the suggestion again of Emma's sister Madame Louise Bouvier. The new governess was born in Ireland and had benefited from a European education that concentrated on literature and language. From the start she took complete charge of the girls' education and supervised the others who served on the faculty. Her influence on the children went far beyond their classical education. She was a woman of profound religious faith and she shared her enthusiasm for Christian living with the whole Drexel family. From a devout Irish Catholic family she instilled in her charges the important role that devotion to God should play in their lives. She gave them the example of that devotion in the way she lived.

The governess selected a group of outstanding teachers to assist her in the instruction of her bright and talented pupils. The most prominent instructor of music in the area, Professor Michael Cross, was chosen to teach piano and to instill a love and enthusiasm for music. The professor was assisted by the children's father. An accomplished pianist, often in the evening before bedtime he would entertain his family with concerts of classical music.

The love of language was also an important part of their schooling. Miss Justine Clave took charge teaching the French language. As a result of her efforts all the Drexel children became fluent in French and had many opportunities to use their knowledge especially on their European trips.

Miss Cassidy felt that an appreciation of the classics required a knowledge of Latin. Professor Allen, the co-author of the world renowned *Allen and Greenough Grammar*, was chosen to tutor the children in Latin. Katie showed a special interest in and talent for the Latin classics and demonstrated a love for the language of the Church throughout her religious life.

The talented governess had a truly vivacious personality and sparked the interest of her young students. She had a unique teaching method. She insisted that thoughts and ideas should be put into writing. Every class that she conducted included as homework that the children spend some time to summarize the lesson in an essay, a poem or a story. In this way she preserved a record of their progress and they provided the world with a record of almost every word that Katharine Drexel ever wrote on paper. They are preserved for us in the Archives of the Sisters of the Blessed Sacrament at their motherhouse in Cornwells Heights, Pennsylvania.

The teaching provided by the governess and her associates offered the girls the best of a liberal arts education. They were taught to think in a logical fashion and to grow in their love for the arts, especially literature and music. The children responded with enthusiasm and tried to make their teachers proud of them with their literary efforts. Their first Christmas together,

Katie suggested that they send their teacher a community Christmas card. With great ceremony they presented the card to Miss Cassidy who read it aloud to the family:

> "A Xmas ever merry;
> A Christmas ever bright;
> How many breaths will smell of sherry
> In this Yule's festive light."

Mrs. Drexel took an active role in the program of studies and took special delight in conducting a series of Sunday night sessions devoted to a discussion of the lives of saints. She helped instill in her children a fascination for heroes of our faith. She frequently led the discussions and encouraged family members to take part. In this way they developed a knowledge of their own patron saints and shared this devotion with other members of the family.

At these Sunday sessions Katie became especially fond of St. Francis of Assisi and delighted in telling the story of his renouncing the riches and honors of the world and the development of his genuine concern for the poorest of God's children. This devotion to Francis remained with her throughout her life. In many ways she imitated him by trying to alleviate the poverty and correct the injustices done to the blacks and Native Americans in her own day. As he was willing to give away his large inheritance to the poor of his day, so she would be willing to give away her inherited millions to those who suffered injustice in her day.

Devotion to God's saints became an important part of her personal prayer life and throughout her life she encouraged her sisters to pattern their lives after their examples. Mrs. Drexel's Sunday sessions had a direct effect on the lives of dedicated religious for many years.

Not to be outdone by his wife, Francis Drexel involved himself in imparting on his children a love for the history and the geography of America. Each fall at the beginning of another school year he planned extensive trips to places of historical significance or natural beauty. Before they made their trips to Europe he wanted to make sure that the girls had firsthand knowledge of their native land. In planning the trip he would read about the areas and give his charges a running commentary on each place they visited.

Perhaps at the insistence of Miss Cassidy, he required that his students write down in essay form their impressions of the places they visited during these historic trips. In the years before their first trip abroad in 1874, they visited the White Mountains and the coast of Maine in the east; New Orleans in the south; the area of the Great Lakes and in the far west Colorado and California.

The family agreed that the days spent in the White Mountains were the most impressive of all the places they saw on the vacation trip. Katie, in a letter to Miss Cassidy , said that she hated to leave the mountains. She reported what she felt about them in these words, "No sunset makes these peaks soft. They never melt into the heavens as some mountains do. But they remind me in their might of eternity—the time that was, the time that will be."

When Katie was twelve Francis Drexel purchased a farm in the town of Torresdale. The large piece of property included ninety acres of land and a huge farmhouse. He decided to renovate the old building as a place where the family could spend the summer months and escape the heat of the city. In addition to the large house, he built a series of cottages for servants and guests and an enormous stable for the family horses. The farm lands were converted to a series of flower beds containing a large variety of blooms. The result of all his efforts was in the words of Emma Drexel, " A gallery of breathtaking beauty."

His extensive renovation took more than a year. In June of 1871 the family moved to the summer estate to enjoy the natural beauty of the Pennsylvania countryside. The property came to mean a great deal to the family and later on to the Congregation of Sisters of the Blessed Sacrament.

The house was more than 150 years old. Its French owners named it in honor of St. Michael the Archangel. A large stone statue of the saint had been erected over the main entrance to the building. As you entered the building, there was a large stained glass window fitted into an alcove at the top of the main flight of stairs. Literally and figuratively, St. Michael dominated the scene and became a special patron for the new owners of the estate. In writing to a friend, Mrs. Drexel spoke of the role of their patron in these words, "St. Michael is the angel of the nativity, the passion, the resurrection and the ascension of Our Lord. I have read a legend that said when Mary left her body, it was St. Michael who received her and carried her up to heaven."

As religion played an important role in the house on Walnut Street, so it would assume an equally important place in their new country home. Within the first few months after her arrival, the lady of the house established what she called a "Sunday School." She realized that there were many young people, children of those who worked on the estate, who had little knowledge of their Catholic faith. Mrs. Drexel asked her two older daughters (ages 14 and 12) to conduct weekly discussions about the role of God in the lives of the young.

From the beginning, these classes met every Sunday afternoon. Elizabeth cared for the younger children and Katharine instructed the children who had received First Communion. After the children finished their weekly lesson, they were brought into the living room to gather around the piano and sing popular hymns of the day. In later years Louise wrote about these sessions and reported that after a few years, there were fifty children who were members of the Drexel Sunday School. When St. Michael's House was closed for the season, a party was held and prizes were awarded to the best students and those with the best attendance. For many years the children were invited back at Christmas time for a special celebration.

The older Drexel children were very conscientious about their teaching responsibilities. For the rest of her life Katharine extended herself to share her faith with others especially with disadvantaged minority groups. She gave her life and her fortune to teach her Native and African American brothers and sisters about God and his Church.

The children enjoyed their stay in their country home which lacked the formality of their Walnut Street house. In the city everything was so formal. At meals, a butler stood at the door and servants prepared and served the meal to family and guests who were formally attired. Their home furnishings were costly and elaborate. The quality of the cuisine served was well known to the social elite of the city.

St. Michael's, on the other hand, was much more to their liking. Katie, especially, enjoyed the more carefree and relaxed atmosphere of the country.

On summer mornings, often the whole family would accompany Francis to the dock where he boarded the boat for his daily trip to Philadelphia. He was joined by the other well-to-do businessmen who lived in the Torresdale area. Each afternoon they came back to the country in their comfortable paddle wheeler.

While their father was at his desk at the bank, the children had a great deal of free time which they spent to their advantage. They were encouraged by their mother to read and to practice French with their friends. They quickly made friends with the young people who lived in the neighborhood. The area was made up of very large estates that were occupied by wealthy and well educated families who were interested in the arts. The children who played together were of much the same temperament. They became lifelong friends and had a good influence on each other. It was a unique environment for the adults and children as well.

As she had done in their city home, Mrs. Drexel set out to make St. Michael's a special place for prayer and worship. She supervised the construction of a family oratory. Carefully she selected the altar, the statues and other appointments for the sanctuary. She succeeded in creating a comfortable room for family prayer. Often the family would gather for prayer and the reading of the scripture. It became a favorite place for Katie to spend some quiet time writing a journal that usually included resolutions for the future. Her notebooks from these days indicate that she had reached a high level of spiritual maturity at a very tender age. The oratory made an ideal place for these literary efforts.

When the oratory was completed, Francis asked his friend Archbishop Wood to come to St. Michael's and bless the new sanctuary. The family and some friends from the neighborhood gathered on a beautiful September morning as the archbishop celebrated Mass and blessed the oratory. He praised the faith of the family that led them to the construction of this place for prayer and he gave the unusual permission that Mass might be celebrated in the oratory four times a year. The family was delighted with this privilege.

Accompanying the archbishop on his visit to St. Michael's was the local pastor, Father James O'Connor. He had served as the rector of St. Michael's Seminary in Pittsburgh and was now the pastor of St. Dominic Church in Holmesburg, the church where the Drexel family worshiped. He was a priest who was well known for work with area young people. He served as the spiritual advisor of many seminarians and young women preparing for the religious life.

Father O'Connor quickly became a close family friend. He often came to Francis for financial advice and help. That first day they met, Katie confided in the priest and began a spiritual relationship that would be lifelong. As a young teenage girl she wrote to him asking help in making decisions about her prayer life. More than any other person, as her spiritual director, he would influence her choice of a religious vocation. His dedicated life of service on behalf of disadvantaged Native Americans encouraged her to follow his example and to dedicate her life to the needs of oppressed minorities in her country.

Following the Mass in the new oratory, the archbishop and pastor discussed with the family President Ulysses S. Grant and his newly formulated peace plan. The president had offered a controversial plan that urged the Christian education of Native Americans as a way to solve the problem of their refusal to obey government regulations. They spoke with the Drexels because it was well known that in the past they had given generously to causes to help alleviate the suffering and neglect of indigenous people.

Francis and Emma were ready to offer their support of the president's initiative. At 13 Katie was too young to understand what the implications of all this were, but later in her life she would look back to that breakfast as the start of what would become for her a lifelong calling to service. She and the soon-to-be Bishop O'Connor of Omaha, Nebraska, would become driving forces behind the growing movement of Catholic Social Action that would influence for good the lives of their disadvantaged brothers and sisters.

During the next few years Katie and her sisters would continue to grow spiritually and intellectually in the Drexel Family School. As a result of the shining example of their parents and the guidance of the ever faithful Miss Cassidy, they were becoming bright and articulate Christian teenagers.

# CHAPTER 3

## TEENAGERS ABROAD

The Drexel family had become just about the wealthiest family in all of Philadelphia. Their children were accustomed to having servants at their beck and call and to have their every need cared for. Their mother constantly reminded them of their social responsibilities, but there was no doubt they lived a privileged life. One of the privileges of the wealthy was the grand tour of Europe.

In the last part of the nineteenth century, it was part of the education process that teenagers of well-to-do families spend some time with their parents visiting the major cities of western Europe. So it was to be with Katharine and her family. It is hard to imagine how a businessman could afford to take the time off to bring his entire family on an extensive tour of the cultural and religious shrines of the continent. In the case of the Drexels, extensive tour meant from September of 1874 until the end of May in 1875—nine months of continuous traveling.

During their earlier years the family covered a large part of their own country visiting the important places in American history. Their father was determined to provide them with the opportunity to broaden their horizons by spending some time in Italy, Austria, Switzerland, England, France and Germany.

The whole family, including the nanny Johanna Ryan, embarked on the *Scotia*, the flagship of the Cunard Line. Miss Cassidy, who hesitated to give her approval of the long trip, decided to remain behind to take care of affairs in Philadelphia. Because her charges were about to miss seven or eight months of study, she insisted the girls send her their journals describing in great detail their observations about the things they saw and the people they met. As a result there are volumes that if put together in book-form would provide the world with a good idea of how 19th century teenagers viewed the cradle of western civilization. When she received these journals, Miss Cassidy went over them with a critical eye and let her students know what she thought of them.

England was their first stop and it was a brief one because they planned a return visit. They confined their time to the environs of Westminster Abbey, its chapels and the royal tombs. Johanna, displaying her Irish heritage at the grave of Queen Elizabeth I, remarked, "I just wonder where she is now."

Wanting to tour Switzerland before the snow and cold weather set in, they hurried on to Geneva in October. They marveled at the beauty of the area. In their tour of the mountains and lakes, Katharine enjoyed the scenery and had the opportunity to practice her knowledge of the French language. She became so skilled at it that later on in her trip, much to her delight, she was able to go to Confession in her adopted language. When hearing of it, Miss Cassidy was pleased.

The girls did not seem so impressed with the countryside of Germany and Austria. Outside of the sunset on Lake Lucerne which deeply impressed her, Katharine reported in her journal that "the landscapes we had seen in America were every bit as impressive." Her method of "telling it like it is" makes interesting reading. All of her journals of their European tour are available in the archives at St. Elizabeth Convent in Cornwells Heights. They tell us a lot about her honesty and her deep appreciation of all of God's gifts to her and to her family.

They spent the Feast of the Immaculate Conception in Florence. They were impressed how the people celebrated this holy day. All the stores and businesses were closed for the celebration. The only places open were the churches. On Christmas Eve they reached the city of Naples. While mother took care of Lizzie, the older children and their father spent the early evening shopping. Delighted with the great selection of toys and clothes, Kate picked out a mechanical mouse for her young sister. Despite the joyful Naples celebration, all the family did miss the huge tree that was always a part of their Philadelphia Christmas observance.

Just before New Year's Day, the Drexel family reached Rome. They spent several days sight-seeing in the Eternal City. Before they left home Miss Cassidy had described the shrines and holy places and Kate and her sisters viewed with awe the Vatican treasures and St. Peter's Basilica.

The highlight of the European trip was an audience with the Holy Father, Pope Pius IX. Even their usually very sedate father was excited at the prospect. At the suggestion of a priest friend they decided to give the Holy Father a white, silk skullcap. Little Lizzie was chosen to make the presentation to the pope. Looking up she spoke to him her memorized greeting in sing-song French. She said the prepared words, *"Saint Pere, voulez-vous acceptez cette calotte?"* Then she added her own personal, unrehearsed request, *"Et me donner la votre?"*

The family was shocked by the second request. The pope smiled and said to the little girl, "Why do you want my hat? What would you do with it? Would you put it in your pocket?"

Her answer was "No, no Holy Father, Father. I want to take it home to Philadelphia." With that a smiling Pio Nono took off his skullcap and tossed it in the air so as to land on Lizzie's head. The pope, with a smile on his face, moved on to the next group of pilgrims. Of the astonished Drexels, only Kate had the presence of mind to call out, *"Merci! Merci!"*

The family was so pleased with their Roman interlude that they prolonged their visit for some extra days. Kate was especially reluctant to leave the Eternal City. For the first time on their trip she was deeply impressed with the holiness so evident in the convents, monasteries and shrines. She kept talking her father into spending a little more time in those holy places.

Only when Francis Drexel explained that their next stop would be the Shrine of Our Lady of Lourdes, would Kate leave Rome. In doing so she asked her father if they could come back again some day soon.

She looked forward with high expectations as they made the train ride to the city of Toulouse. She told her sisters years later how much she enjoyed the carriage that took the family to the town of Lourdes and its beautiful shrine. In 1875 it was indeed a beautiful sight. In those early days the grotto lacked the commercialism of a later day. It was in 1862 at the direction of the bishop of Tarbes that the gothic church and beautiful marble statue of Our Lady were constructed. After the bishop's approval of the apparition and the conclusion of the Franco-Prussian War in 1872, pilgrimages to the grotto began. The Drexel family were among the first of what would be a large army of pilgrims who would make the pilgrimage to this holy place to honor Our Lady of Lourdes. On that early February day, for Katharine and her family it was a pilgrimage to walk up the path to the place where the Virgin had appeared. It was a simple shrine, a holy place.

Along the path were countless numbers of candles burning in testimony of the gratitude and faith of those who had come before her. As she reached the grotto she was overcome by the beauty of the statue of Our Lady of Lourdes. When the other members of the family reached the sanctuary, she told them of the words of Bernadette as she spoke of the statue which was formed from her description of the Beautiful Lady of the apparition. Bernadette put it this way, *"C'est belle mais ce n'est pas elle."* ("It is beautiful but not as beautiful as she is.")

The holiness of Lourdes and the simple grotto had a profound effect on the young visitor from America. She read again the story of what happened there and of the hundreds who claimed to be cured through the intervention of the Mother of God.

Later Louise would report to Miss Cassidy that her sister was so moved by what she saw and read about the shrine that, as they drove away, she leaned out the back of their carriage with a tear in her eye to watch the grotto church disappear in the distance.

It was Lent when they reached Paris. In the City of Lights there were two big attractions for the teenage tourists—one was a Dominican priest, Pere Olivier—and the other Paris' most famous department store Worth's. The whole family enjoyed the popular Lenten orator and they went to hear him speak at the Cathedral of Notre Dame on several occasions.

The girls were especially impressed because he spoke so clearly that despite their limited knowledge of formal French they could understand his every word. Katharine was especially moved by his message as he invited his hearers to follow more closely in the footsteps of Jesus during the holy season of Lent. Apparently many who attended agreed with the Drexel family. The congregation grew so large that before Lent was over the cathedral rector decided to charge admission to come to hear the famous orator.

They carefully took notes from his sermons and sent them home to Miss Cassidy. She congratulated them for their knowledge of French and for their interest in things of the Spirit. His messages were remembered by the older girls and they spoke of them years later.

Their experiences at Worth's Department Store were far different. Their mother had prepared them for what was to be an exciting day. For Katharine it was very tiring and she had little interest in most of the things being sold. Mrs. Drexel was pleased with the way they were treated in the famous store, but it was a different story for the young people. They had little difficulty understanding the French language the salespeople spoke, but they were very unhappy about their attitude in dealing with their young customers.

In particular Katharine had some harsh words. In her letter to Miss Cassidy she expressed her displeasure with these unusual comments about her experiences. "I am afraid," she said, "that the contact that my corrupt nature has recently suffered from these Parisian torments has made me imbibe their extreme want of exactness if not their mealymouthedness." She then compared the treatment they received in the Paris store with the attitude and much more friendly atmosphere in Wanamaker's, their favorite shopping place in Philadelphia.

Her teacher was surprised by the unusual harshness of her commentary but admired the honesty with which she made her appraisal of her unhappy experience. Throughout her life Katharine would always be honest in telling about things as she saw them.

Winding up their extended European tour, the family crossed the channel to visit England in the springtime. Before they left home their governess had prepared a list of historic places to visit. By this time it was April and May and the countryside was most beautiful. They would have perhaps liked to have spent more time viewing the English landscape, but they dutifully visited the places that Miss Cassidy had selected for them.

Their most interesting stop was at the Tower of London. Before leaving on their trip, Katharine had spent a great deal of time reading about the life and times of the English Jesuit priest John Gerard. He is best known as one of the few prisoners who ever escaped from the infamous tower prison. She was determined to see for herself the prison cell in which he was detained and the window from which he came by rope to the wharf below.

Actually the prison is not one but a series of small towers and fortresses. When they came to the Cradle Tower where Gerard was held prisoner, they were told that part of the prison was not open to visitors. Katharine was incensed. She shouted at their guide, "I suppose that you people are ashamed to let us see the dirty black hole your ancestors put Father John in to torture him." Her protest was to no avail and the group left the Tower of London without ever seeing the famous prison cell.

They had a much more enjoyable time in the world famous British Museum. They spent several days looking over the impressive exhibits. Miss Cassidy was pleased to receive several interesting essays from her pupils. Katharine wrote with great delight about the Rossetta Stone and the examples of ancient Egyptian papyri. They were also enthralled with the well-known manuscripts that were on display. Lizzie quotes these caustic words of her older sister Katharine concerning the writings of Martin Luther. After reading the manuscript she was reported to have said, "Look at that mean and scrawny piece of handwriting." Neither Miss Cassidy nor her parents approved of her comments.

By the time the Drexels finished their visit to England, it was the middle of May. Francis intended that their tour would include the countries of Ireland and Scotland. The family talked it over and decided that they had seen enough and were anxious to get home to their country house now that the good weather had begun.

Upon their arrival back in Philadelphia, the Drexel family discussed the trip with Johanna Ryan and Miss Cassidy. All agreed that the children had matured a great deal. They were especially impressed by their new writing skills and their ability to clearly convey their thoughts in their conversations with adults. All agreed that the nine months spent in Europe had added much to their liberal arts education. Even their demanding teacher admitted that they could not have learned as much if they had spent that nine months in her Philadelphia classroom.

By early June the Drexel girls were back teaching Sunday School to the younger children on their Torresdale estate.

Katharine Drexel at age 16.

# CHAPTER 4

# COMING OF AGE

Following their months of touring the great sites of Europe, the family was happy to resume life in the countryside at St. Michael's. Quickly they got into their summertime mode with their neighbors and friends in Torresdale. The summer months passed quickly and in early fall the children returned to the Drexel Family School on Walnut Street.

Almost immediately after their return to Philadelphia they became involved in the preparation for the coming celebration of the 100th anniversary of the Declaration of Independence. The city was to be the center of a year-long celebration. The Drexels played a special role in the festivities and hosted many patriotic parties.

The celebration began on New Year's Eve. The city was aglow with lights. Bands and party-goers crowded the streets. The whole Drexel family and their servants were in the streets enjoying the patriotic flavor of the centennial party. Katharine was disappointed when her tired father directed his family home more than an hour before the midnight celebration began. Much to her dismay they were safely in their beds when the Centennial Year of 1876 began.

This is Katharine's journal description of how the New Year's Eve party ended. "We sat up in our beds till the last peals of the bells died away, wishing we were at Independence Hall to see the hoisting of the United States Flag, and then I blush to say that we spontaneously sunk in our pillows not even to dream of the old patriots whose heroic love of country caused liberty to be rung throughout the land, nearly one hundred years ago."

In many ways Katharine Drexel was a woman of her time. She was proud to be an American. A young woman of immense wealth, she recognized her Christian obligation of service to others. While she lived in the social whirl of 19th century Philadelphia society, she set her heart on higher things. More and more she began to ponder what she would do with her life.

The year marking the 100th anniversary of the nation passed quickly. The rash of parties and parades and celebrations wreaked havoc with Miss Cassidy's schedule of classes. Time after time she had to excuse the popular Drexel girls because of their busy social schedule. Many at the Walnut Street house heaved a sigh of relief when the year finally came to an end.

During this period Katharine pursued the writing of journals and essays. She kept notes on her meditations, her retreats and her resolutions for the future. More and more her journals concentrated on spiritual matters and less and less were concerned with secular activities. Much time was spent in communicating with her spiritual director. She often sought his advice and reported to him her successes and her failures.

One of the most significant events of the centennial year was the departure of Father O'Connor from the archdiocese of Philadelphia. The Holy Father recognized his ability and his long felt desire to devote his life to work with Native Americans. He was consecrated a bishop and sent to Omaha, Nebraska. He assumed a huge responsibility and his territory included all of Nebraska and parts of five other states in the western part of our country.

Katharine was pleased that her spiritual father had been raised to the hierarchy but disappointed that he would move two thousand miles away. Since she was twelve years old, he had been there to guide and help her through the difficult years of coming of age. They had developed a deep spiritual relationship and she was fearful of the future without his direction. Before he left to assume his new post, he visited with the Drexel family and explained to them that he would still be available with his friendship and advice. He reassured Katharine and explained to her that "My going so far away doesn't mean that I'm giving up my spiritual child."

Bishop O'Connor promised that he would return to Philadelphia from time to time and that he would write to her often and answer her questions and continue to share his advice. In the coming years he kept that promise. His many letters described his work and encouraged the Drexels to come to Nebraska to see firsthand the important work of his apostolate.

In addition to her correspondence with the bishop, there are available many of her personal notebooks and spiritual diaries. At the end of a retreat or the start of a new year she would describe in detail her resolutions for the future and then keep a record of efforts to live up to her spiritual goals. On New Year's Eve of 1881, she wrote these words of resolution, "Dear Little Infant Jesus, by your humble crib I make these resolutions for the coming year in the presence of the Blessed Virgin. No cake for the year. No preserves until June. No grapes and honey until July 1st."

During this period she was difficult with herself as she examined her conscience and admitted to her faults. Never really discouraged by her lack of progress, her journals indicate that over the years she developed into a young woman who accepted her calling to live a more perfect life and with the help of her spiritual director was looking forward to dedicating her life to the Lord. She had not determined exactly how she would do this.

The days of classroom study came to an end for Katharine in the spring of 1878. She had adapted well to the program of studies. Miss Cassidy and her other teachers were confident that she was ready to begin an adult life in the real world. At the age of twenty she was prepared to take her place in the late 19th century society of her native city. She was looking forward to the big night at which her family would formally introduce her to that society. The date for her debut was January 1, 1879.

The night of one's formal debut was a momentous occasion in the life of any young woman whose family held an important place in society. Francis and Emma Drexel were among the wealthiest and most powerful people in all of Philadelphia society. Their eldest daughter Elizabeth had made her debut the previous year and that coming out was the topic of discussion throughout the winter season. The debut of Katharine was anticipated as the social event of the 1879 social calendar.

It is hard for us to determine what making her debut really meant to the young debutante. In a letter to her spiritual director just a week after the event, after a description of her holiday activities, she mentioned it in passing by saying that "I attended a little party the other night where I made my debut."

That "little party" was attended by just about every prominent family in town. The huge drawing room of the family mansion on Walnut Street was beautifully decorated. Katharine, her parents and her older sister stood by the hour to formally greet all their distinguished guests. The local papers described the evening in great detail. They reported that she looked radiant in a beautiful white gown that Worth's Department Store had created especially for the occasion. The guest of honor paused to speak to each one who had come to welcome her with a poise and bearing that delighted everyone in the receiving line. It was truly a smashing evening.

Katharine seemed delighted with herself and her party. As the last of the hundreds of guests were leaving, she threw herself into the arms of her parents and is reported to have exclaimed, "Oh, I just love parties. I truly love them. I am never going to stop going to parties for as long as I live."

Following the elaborate debut there was a flurry of social activity for Katharine and Elizabeth. They were guests at countless parties. As usual in the spring they went to their country home. During the season they made many visits to Long Branch, Cape May and other vacation places and summer homes along the Jersey shore. At each of the get togethers they were the guests of honor. At all of the parties there was a great amount of matchmaking plans that were devised by their family and friends. Throughout the summer months a huge array of eligible suitors sought to impress them.

Bishop O'Connor wrote to Katharine to congratulate her on her coming out. He said that he was pleased that she was so popular but also reminded her of her Christian responsibilities. He talked to her of the good example given by her parents who lived lives spent for God in a social setting where He was often ignored.

Some of the happiest times during this social summer were the days spent at the home of George Childs who was the publisher of the *Philadelphia Ledger*. He and his wife were like members of the family and were called aunt and uncle. They welcomed the debutantes to their luxurious summer home at Sea Cliff. Here the young ladies met all kinds of people of different ages and professions, all of them wealthy and influential in the community.

Their parents were delighted that the girls were meeting such important and interesting friends. Francis wrote to them in Sea Cliff and said how much he missed them not being at St. Michael's but "We willingly bear your absence when we know that you are enjoying yourselves." His wife agreed with him and wrote these words to her children: "I am anxious to have you lose no opportunity for gaining world experience and you will have one hundred times more opportunity of meeting persons there than when at home."

The summer of 1879 was a happy time for the two girls. They thoroughly enjoyed their trips and the new friends that had become part of their lives. They came home in August to a family who had truly missed them. When they returned to Torresdale, Elizabeth told their parents about all the interesting people they met and how popular her sister was at all of the celebrations. She reported that "Everywhere we went Katharine was an instant social success and loved by all."

The girls were not home long when it became clear that their mother was not feeling well. Katharine told her mother that she looked thin and was not her cheerful self. Emma brushed her off by saying that it was a hot summer and too much gardening and riding caused her to lose some weight.

As the weeks went on she became weaker and the smallest chore wore her out. She did her best to conceal her failing health from those she loved. She consulted a doctor who told her that she needed a minor operation to remove the cause of her ever growing severe pains. She refused to go to the hospital but agreed to meet the doctor at her home on Walnut Street. Amazing as it may seem even in 1879, the operation was performed right in her home and it was a disaster. The doctor discovered that a malignant cancerous growth was the cause of her suffering.

When Francis discovered what had happened , he was devastated. He rushed to Philadelphia to see her. His eyes filled with tears as he asked her, "Emma, Emma, oh why did you let anyone do this to you?"

She tried to explain to him that she did not want to cause her family to be concerned over her condition and thought that the operation would solve her medical problem. In an effort to save her life, during the coming months Francis called in the best medical help available. After many examinations and consultations it was determined that nothing could be done except to try to make her as comfortable as possible.

During the fall and winter months her pain and suffering grew more intense. During these difficult months Katharine more and more assumed the responsibility of caring for her very ill mother. She loved her very much and was glad to make any sacrifice on her behalf. During the next two years she spent many hours at her mother's side. Though there were servants available and professional nurses, she insisted on being at her side whenever possible. It disturbed her to see the pain in her mother's face and she did everything possible to relieve her suffering. Later, it is recorded in the annals of her congregation, she told her religious sisters that the suffering of her mother made her realize the gravity of original sin that brought suffering and death into the world.

The suffering and eventual death of her mother had a profound effect on her life. More than ever she realized that the Lord had sent her to help relieve suffering and provide for the needs of those who lived in pain and had to depend on others for their basic needs. Throughout her adult life she willingly gave of herself in the service of others and recruited hundreds of religious women who would follow in her footsteps.

Mrs. Drexel suffered a long and painful illness. Well known doctors used their most effective drugs and additional surgery. At several points they reduced her pain and she seemed to improve. In the summer of 1880 the family took a specially planned trip to Colorado but returned home because she was uncomfortable traveling.

In 1881 the family journeyed to the White Mountains. They spent a quiet summer in a rustic cabin cut off from the business world. They returned in the fall and spent the holidays at St. Michael's. It was not a happy Christmas because during this period she was suffering greatly.

The next summer the family traveled to Sharon Springs, New York. While there Mrs. Drexel seemed to improve again enjoying the water and the sulphur springs. They returned to

Philadelphia just before Christmas and she took a turn for the worse. Her last month on earth she was in terrible pain. At one point she told her husband, "O Frank, how I pray that when your time comes , you will be spared all this, and now I offer this pain I suffer for you."

As Katharine sat by her bedside and saw her mother's beautiful sense of resignation to God's will, she spoke to her grieving father about her thoughts about the religious life and how she wished to dedicate her life to God. It was during these moments that a religious vocation became a realistic goal for her.

On January 29, 1883 at her family home in Philadelphia, Mrs. Emma Drexel died. The family was overwhelmed with grief. The entire community mourned her passing. In an editorial the *Philadelphia Ledger* editorialized, "The hundreds who passed through her home for a mournful farewell were largely composed of those to whom she had been a benefactress. Their sorrow was unmistakable."

In a memorial booklet, Philadelphia poet Eleanor Donnelley penned these words in her memory:

"No golden shrine all gem-bespent
Fame o'er your ashes rears.
Behold the poor—your monument!
Your epitaph—their tears!"

In the spring the family returned to their summer home as usual. The summer proved to be a time to mourn. Filled with grief, Francis decided to take his daughters on a brief European trip to distract them from their grief. The family left in October and visited Holland, Italy, France and England. It was in the Cathedral at Venice where Katharine had attended Mass that a strange incident occurred. As she received Communion a server handed her a holy card that contained a picture of the Madonna and Child. For some strange reason it caused her to think of the day when the whole family gathered around her suffering mother and Katharine suddenly blurted out, "If anything happens to Mamma, I'm going to enter a convent." Her sisters were amused by the remark but all quickly forgot about it.

Reminded of the event in the Venice cathedral, Katharine took the card and for years kept it in her prayer book. That night she wrote in her diary, "I don't know why but that card put all the old convent ideas back in my mind."

Katharine communicated her renewed interest in the religious life in a long and thoughtful letter to her spiritual director in Nebraska.

Katharine at age 21.

# CHAPTER 5

## THE WILL

On the trip back to America, Katharine often thought of the possibility of life in a contemplative convent. She was very impressed during their brief visit in Siena with the Dominican convent, the home of St. Catherine. She was delighted to read that the saint of Siena was a woman of intense prayer and one who found time to work among the sick and lonely in the city. On her return home, she decided to discuss the whole matter with her spiritual director. Little did she know that their paths, as if by divine command, would cross soon after her arrival home.

While they were in Europe, Francis' friend Archbishop Wood had died. Bishop O'Connor wrote to them telling them that a good friend of his, Bishop Patrick Ryan from St. Louis, had been appointed by the pope to be the new Archbishop of Philadelphia. The Drexel family was invited to attend the ceremony of the installation of the new archbishop in the cathedral church. Francis and Katharine represented the family at the Episcopal installation. The three-hour ceremony was attended by scores of bishops and priests from throughout the country. As they marched down the aisle, Francis pointed out one of the bishops that he thought looked like Bishop O'Connor, their friend from Nebraska.

When they reached the bishop's house for the reception, they were delighted to see Bishop O'Connor, who had come to the city with the new archbishop. He told the Drexels of the tumultuous welcome given Archbishop Ryan at the railroad station. Thousands of the faithful lined the streets as the bishop's carriage passed to shouts of welcome.

After the ceremonies Katharine was delighted to have the opportunity to spend some time in conversation with her spiritual director. She told him how difficult it was to express her thoughts on paper. From her letters and their conversations the bishop knew much about the depths of her faith and the intensity of her personal prayer life.

The archives tell us of this important conversation about Katharine and her potential religious vocation. First he told her of the life of the sisters working with him in the famous Rosebud Reservation. He explained how hard the sisters worked and how successful they were in opening boarding schools.

Then Katharine explained that she had some important questions to talk to him about. She let him know that during her trip to Europe, she thought a great deal about her future. In Venice and Siena, especially, she felt she was being called to join the convent. Clearly the bishop was not surprised. During recent months she often hinted at this possibility. At this face-to-face meeting she clearly verbalized her thoughts and looked to her spiritual director for some advice about what to do.

To her great surprise, instead of answering her question about whether or not she should enter the religious life, he asked her a question. He thought for a few moments and then prayerfully asked, "Is it the active life you are thinking about, my child?" Startled by the question, she shook her head. With conviction she answered, "No. No. I would want to enter a contemplative order of nuns. I am afraid that you are going to tell me that I have to have some real evidence that it is God's will for me before I can enter that life. Please tell me what I should do—enter now or wait?"

The bishop did not have an immediate answer to that question. He pondered it for a few days. Just before leaving for Nebraska, he told her how he felt. The bishop directed her to "Wait a little longer. Wait and pray."

Reluctantly, Katharine agreed to do as he said. The summer of 1884 was spent at St. Michael's. They tried to resume their normal pattern of living. Emma had taught her daughters well. Each assumed the responsibilities and duties she had laid out for them as she prepared for the day she would not be with them. In the fall, Francis decided that it would be good for the family to join him on a business trip through the great Northwest. With a certain degree of enthusiasm they began their last journey with their father.

They traveled in style. The Northern Pacific Railroad offered for their use their most prestigious private car, The Yellowstone. The reason why the leaders of Drexel Company were taking the trip was to decide whether or not the Northern Pacific would be a good investment for the bank. Along with the banking team, the girls' cousin Mary Dixon, who had also lost her mother, was invited on the trip. The four girls enjoyed each other's company and the train ride helped them over a difficult period of mourning. Katharine recorded what happened in detail—the trip from St. Michael's to Portland, Oregon and back covered exactly 6,838 miles. She never explained exactly how she arrived at this precise number.

For the girls the best part of the trip was a special stopover to visit Yellowstone National Park. It was here that Mr. Drexel and his distinguished banking friends were arrested for theft. The day before the arrest, the state of Wyoming passed a law making it illegal to remove from the territory a single object, be it plant or mineral. There was no doubt that the Drexel family had a beautiful collection of valuable minerals in their possession. Their trial took place in the village before a justice of the peace. They were finally exonerated when officials from Yellowstone Park told the judge that the minerals were gifts from the park authority. The bankers and the girls learned a lesson that day about frontier justice.

The journey home had only one stop in Chicago. The bankers conducted some business there and the girls went shopping in the brand new Marshall Field's Department Store. Their stay in the Windy City ended with a trip down Drexel Boulevard which was named in honor of the girls' grandfather who had done a great deal of business there.

Shortly after their arrival back from the Northwest Territory, things began to return to a degree of normalcy at the Walnut Street house. One day Francis came home from work early with a great surprise for his daughters. He gathered them into a parlor and told them that he left early because he had completed a good day's work. When Elizabeth asked what that good work might be, her father said with a smile of satisfaction, "I have made out my last will and testament."

His children were shocked. There were some anxious tears. Quickly the father assured them that he was feeling fine and there was no emergency. He explained that he made out his will with the help of some of his banking associates to safeguard their futures and the futures of their children. In recent months several of his friends' children had been the victims of fortune hunters who squandered their estates. He was determined that the money he worked so hard to obtain would provide for the needs of his beloved family for generations. He thought that his will was a guarantee that his earnings would remain safely in the Drexel family for years to come. Somehow the Lord had different ideas.

He sought the help of the best known lawyers and bankers in the country. He spent long hours putting together what would become one of the most talked about wills in all of history. Three times it received national publicity and was the object of much discussion in the press at the time of his death in 1885, at the time of Katharine's death in 1955 and at the time of her canonization in 2000.

In preparation for drawing up the will, Francis appointed as his executives his brother Anthony J. Drexel, a distinguished banker in his own right; his best friend George Childs, the publisher of the *Philadelphia Ledger*; and his brother-in-law, John D. Lankenau, a very successful business leader in the community. They employed the best legal minds available to hammer out the provisions of the will. The text of the will can be found in the Archives. It would take seventy years to determine how the funds were to be distributed. With the death of Katharine, the legacy of more than $14,500,000 was lost to the Drexel Family and the Sisters of the Blessed Sacrament.

The will directed the executors to make a complete inventory of the assets and their real value. Total assets amounted to about $16,000,000. This was an enormous amount of money in 1885. The first provision in Article V directed that 10% of the assets be distributed to 29 charitable, educational and religious institutions. One of the recipients was a Lutheran hospital founded by John Lankenau and his family. All were within the Philadelphia area. This distribution was to be made at the time of his death.

The next article in the will directed that the remaining residuary of the estate should be called the Trust Estate and the annual net income from the trust was to be divided among the three daughters. It stated that if one of the daughters dies childless, her share would go to the other two. If the second also dies childless, the income goes to the third daughter. In this Francis believed that he had provided the best possible means of protecting his estate for his children and grandchildren.

Article VI had one more provision that proved to be the most important of all. It stated that in the remote possibility there were no living children of the three daughters, the entire estate would be divided among the 29 institutions and charities named in the will. This remote possibility became a reality in 1955.

It is estimated that Katharine Drexel, in her lifetime, invested some $20 million in providing for the needs of African and Native Americans. Today it would amount to about $250 million. Because the Sisters of the Blessed Sacrament were not in existence before her father's death, since 1955 they have received no financial help from the Drexel estate. Francis had no idea that his daughter would be the foundress of a religious order of more than five hundred members. There was no way he could have anticipated their great need of funds to continue her work among the disadvantaged.

Katharine lived to be 97 years old. When her younger sister Louise Drexel Morrell died suddenly in 1943, she became the sole remaining beneficiary of her father's will. She realized that after her death her religious community would lose their major source of income. At no point did she ever consider the possibility of trying to break Francis' will.

She determined that she would disburse the interest from the family trust fund to support the charitable work of her congregation for as long as she would live. She respected her father's wishes and believed that American Catholics would come together to provide for continuing the work of her congregation. Frequently in the last years of her life she told her sisters that "You must depend on the providence of God and the generosity of his people."

When she died, the more than $15 million in the trust fund was distributed according to the instructions in the will. Cardinal John F. O'Hare, C.S.C., the archbishop of Philadelphia, requested that the institutions who shared in the bequest make a contribution to the Sisters of the Blessed Sacrament. Some agreed to do so.

The weeks after their trip to the far west were very busy ones for Francis and the members of his firm. The group had grown so large that it was necessary to move out of their office and to build a new building to accommodate their growing business. They were busy making plans to build the first skyscraper in the city. The entire staff was involved in the planning and the moving of their facilities and equipment.

During this period of great activity Francis was working long hours. When he got home late several times his daughters expressed their concern that he looked tired and thin. He convinced them this was not the case but that he was feeling well and anxious to get on with the big move.

On the second anniversary of Emma's death, January 29, the family attended Mass at St. Patrick's Church and prayed for her soul. Two days later Francis made a rare winter trip to St. Michael's. It was a very cold day with blowing snow. As a result of his exposure to the miserable weather, he caught a severe cold which quickly turned to pleurisy. The doctors ordered him to take an extended bed rest. The Drexel girls took up the nursing duties and saw to it that he took his medications at the proper time. Their efficient service got him on the road to recovery in less than two weeks.

Soon he was able to spend some time playing the organ and reading aloud to his nurses. By the weekend of February 15 he was planning to return to work on a limited basis. On Sunday he went to Mass and after a short walk, he sat with Katharine and read aloud from one of his favorite books, *The Newcomes*. As he started to get up, he groaned and fell back in his chair. His face lost its color and he seemed to lose consciousness. His daughter rushed across the square to St. Patrick's Church to get the priest. By the time they arrived home he was already dead.

The news spread quickly. Soon the financial community and all of Philadelphia was in mourning. His charitable concern for the needy had touched the lives of hundreds of his fellow citizens. His new friend Archbishop Ryan celebrated his funeral

Mass. Almost two thousand mourners filled St. Mary's Church to capacity and scores more stood outside in the February cold. It was an enormous tribute and was said to be the largest funeral the city had ever seen.

Tributes poured into the Drexel home from dozens of charitable societies and institutions. In an editorial, the *Philadelphia Inquirer* stated: "He was a banker for the rich and for the poor. His best and truest epitaph would be the simple record of his life." The editor of the *Catholic Standard and Times* wrote: "He never tired of doing good; and he never cared that the world should know of his benefactions."

At the request of his daughters, there was no eulogy at the funeral. They believed his life spoke for itself. Francis was buried next to his wife in the Bouvier vault. The family had sought permission from the archbishop to construct a mortuary chapel at the Sacred Heart Convent, close to St. Michael's. The building was already under construction before Francis died. A beautiful marble altar was set in place and the bodies of Francis and Emma were buried in a crypt under the altar. After the chapel was blessed in July, the daughters moved to their summer home to struggle to resume their lives without their beloved parents.

Since their earliest days the Drexel family had been deeply involved in an effort to alleviate poverty. They generously gave to a host of charitable causes and willingly served on boards that directed how their contributions would be spent. They had opened their home to the needy on a regular basis. Quietly and without fanfare, they lived lives of giving. Their daughters determined to do everything possible to continue this tradition.

The deaths of their parents drew them closer as a family. The oldest daughter Louise stepped forward to guide their efforts. Sister Dolores Lighthouse, in her family history, reports that Louise took her father's place as a member of boards that

directed several Catholic orphan asylums. She realized that
when the children left these orphanages they were not prepared to become productive members of society. She decided
to direct the erection of a trade school to provide the students
with a useful occupation. Her efforts resulted in the construction of St. Francis Industrial School which was named in memory of her father.

This trade school, the first in the area, marked the beginning
of a long series of charitable institutions erected by the Drexel
daughters following a tradition their parents had begun.

A few months after the death of their father, two priests
came to visit the family home. They came as a result of the
national publicity about the huge charitable bequests in the
family will. The three daughters were home when the guests
arrived. As fate or divine intervention would have it, Elizabeth
asked Katharine to go down to the parlor to meet the guests
because neither she nor Louise were properly dressed for the
occasion.

Actually the reason why the two daughters wanted
Katharine to meet the priests had nothing to do with dress.
Katharine was the one most deeply affected by her father's
death. She had been on duty when he was stricken and somehow she blamed herself that the priest was unable to get to him
before he died. Elizabeth wanted to get her sister involved and
thought the priests' project would capture her interest. How
right she was.

The interview with the two priests, Bishop Martin Marty
and Father Joseph Stephan, would change the direction of her
life and provide her with an interest that would be the driving
force of her future apostolate. The bishop was in charge of the
mission church in the Dakota Territory and the priest worked
with the Catholic Indian Bureau.

They told her of their St. Francis Mission on the huge
Rosebud Reservation in South Dakota. They spoke of a school

they wanted to build and how the Franciscan sisters would be willing to staff the school when it was built. Katharine was deeply moved by their message and plea for help. She immediately promised that the Drexel Family would help in the building of the mission school and in other places where the missions needed the most help.

From this point on for the rest of her years she devoted her life as an apostle for human rights and vowed to do all she could to provide for the needs of Native Americans who had been so poorly treated by their fellow citizens. Bishop O'Connor wrote to her about the desperation of his people and the need for priests and sisters to work in his missions. Her meeting with the two priests and her letters from her director helped to fill a void in her life and gave her a unique opportunity to serve the Lord in a mission apostolate.

# CHAPTER 6

# PREPARING FOR A DECISION

Katharine was in failing health. In the past two years she had seen her mother suffer a slow and painful death and her father die, stricken by a sudden attack. Her sisters and extended family were concerned by her jaundiced color and loss of weight. Several prominent doctors were called in to examine the young patient and provide her with different medications. Nothing seemed to help. She continued to lose weight and had little or no energy to do her usual chores. At the end of a year, despite the efforts of her doctors, she was no better.

One of her doctors, Anthony Da Costa, had a private meeting with Elizabeth and suggested they might consider a visit to the famous baths at Schwalbach in Germany. He knew one of the doctors who would see to it that Katharine received the proper treatment. Hearing this she decided to urge her two sisters to join her on a trip to Europe. She was amazed when both of them were delighted to make the trip.

Elizabeth indicated that she wanted to go to the continent to see how the Europeans were using the concept of trade schools to provide orphan boys with the knowledge necessary for them to be productive members of society. She thought that she would be able to use these methods in her new trade school in Philadelphia. Louise was also interested in how the Irish and French constructed their educational facilities for the poor and orphans. Katharine was interested in the trip to help Bishop O'Connor find priests to help in the missions. She intended to seek that help in the convents and monasteries, especially in Italy.

The primary, but perhaps unstated, reason for the European jaunt was to help Katharine to regain her health, energy, and her zest for living.

Francis' brother, Andrew Drexel, accompanied the ladies to the boat. He assumed a fatherly role and came to give his nieces some advice to help them on their journey. An old family servant, Martin, was appointed to watch over them and had the annoying habit of walking exactly twelve yards behind them and never taking part in the conversation. He proved, however, to be of great assistance in obtaining hotel rooms and transportation. The faithful nanny, Johanna Ryan, also accompanied them. She became a kind of chaperon and confidant and a constant source of help. She caused quite a stir among her fellow travelers during their brief stay in her Irish homeland.

With the fatherly advice of their Uncle Anthony ringing in their ears, the entire entourage set sail for Ireland on the *S.S. Ambria* on July 31, 1886 just a little more than one year after the death of their beloved father. The ocean voyage over was a pleasant one. Resting much of the time in her steamer chair with a relaxing and calm sea, Katharine seemed to regain some of her strength and color. After a brief stop in Ireland, the party set out to visit the famous German spa.

Katharine was surely aware of her weakened condition because she readily took part in what her German doctors called *"Kur"* or "the cure." It was a long and certainly not an easy program. She was told at the beginning it would take five weeks and she knew that her sisters would be spending the time visiting many interesting places in the area. While they would be enjoying themselves, under the watchful eyes of Martin and Johanna, she was confined to Schwalbach and the strict regimen of the German doctors in charge. The program included frequent mud baths each day; drinking of the spring water at specific times of the day and daily baths in the spa pools of health-giving water.

The unusual treatment obviously agreed with her. When her sisters returned each evening after their sightseeing trips, they noticed the improvement. Much of the tension left Katharine and her strength was clearly renewed. Before the five-week session was over she became like her own self again. During the last two weeks, she joined her sisters for a while each day.

On September 10, the European tour began in earnest. As usual, Katharine kept a daily diary. Once her period of recuperation at the baths was completed, they did the tour in a regal style, stopping at the first class hotels and dining in the best eating places. It was not all fun and games, however, for they stopped also at educational institutions and at convents and monasteries. She noted in her diary the methods used to provide livelihoods for children who had been deprived of parental support. All the girls made use of this experience in later years when they took part in the construction of schools for the disadvantaged in their own country.

Throughout their tour, they received letters from America. Father Stephan was a faithful correspondent. He wrote long letters, several times a month, giving an itemized account of the expenses of the missions supported by the Drexel family. Katharine came to know in detail the day-to-day problems faced by the missionaries. Father Stephan told her on her return to Philadelphia that "Being in the Indian business and its problems almost seems to be something that is a natural part of your life."

As she learned more and more of the plight of her missionaries, Katharine developed a serious concern for the future of the schools and other institutions she was helping to fund. Her priest friends wrote to her about conditions in the mission schools. At the time they had barely enough sisters available to staff the schools.

Years later she explained how she felt during her tour of Europe. She said that Bishop O'Connor wrote to her about a mission he wished to build in Wyoming. He could find a congregation of sisters to staff the school but he could not find an order of priests that would become involved in the work.

Mother Katharine told a mission convention in 1921 how she felt about this. She told the delegates, "But what could sisters do without a priest? I was willing to give the means to put up the mission buildings, but without a priest to minister to the sisters and the heathens—what's the use?"

During the closing days of her tour, she stopped at several monasteries seeking priests to help in working with Native Americans. She failed to find a religious superior who was willing to make this kind of commitment.

She decided in her own mind that there was only one person in the world who could solve Bishop O'Connor's problem. That person was His Holiness Pope Leo XIII. She made up her mind as they came to Rome and were preparing for a private audience with the pope. The only thing she could do was to ask him for his help.

On January 27, 1887, Katharine Drexel entered the Apostolic Palace to experience the defining moment in her life. She asked the question and received the remarkable answer, "Why not, my child, yourself become a missionary?"

Like Mary, Paul, and Augustine, she paused for a moment and then allowed the Lord to take over the direction of her life.

It is important for us to understand that there was nothing personal about her request for priests to help out in the missions. From all we know it does not seem that she had any intentions of speaking to the Holy Father about her own religious vocation. She could, of course, not ignore his question. What the interview did do was to give closure to the idea of a contemplative vocation and open the door to one of the great missionary efforts in the history of the Church.

The trip to Europe was a greater success than any of the sisters imagined it would be. It accomplished several things: Katharine was restored to good health; much was learned about trade schools and other educational institutions; the sisters had enjoyed places of interest like Spain that they had never visited before; and the Holy Father had asked Katharine a question that she would have to answer.

Shortly after their stay in Rome and brief visits to France, England and Scotland, the three sisters and their companions set out for Philadelphia on the *S.S. Eturia.*

No sooner were they home when the sisters received two important letters—one from Bishop O'Connor and the second from Father Stephan. Both had the same message. They were invitations to come to visit the missions that they were helping to fund. The bishop told them that it was necessary for them to see for themselves the difficulties and the successes of their efforts on behalf of Native Americans who lived in poverty and ignorance. He told them quite frankly that the trip would be different than their recent European tour. There were no fancy hotels, no luxury trains and no gourmet meals.

Katharine encouraged her sisters to accept. After much discussion, the decision was made and in September they boarded the train in their native city and started out to Omaha. They knew it would be a difficult journey but decided that if they were to be of help, it was necessary for them to know the conditions under which the people lived. Bishop O'Connor assured his spiritual child that the difficult trip would help her to discern God's will for her and help her to know what He wanted her to accomplish in her life. For this reason, she was anxious to go.

Their first stop was to be St. Francis Mission in Rosebud. The bishop and priest joined the train for the last miles of the trip. At the last railroad stop they were met by a group of Native American mounted police who brought them horses and what they called a carriage. Elizabeth and Louise were expert horsewomen and led the procession. A little less expert, Katharine joined the priests in the carriage. Actually the carriages were nothing more than an open wagon with no protection from sun or rain. It was a difficult ride—long and tiring. They were exhausted when they finally arrived at the mission outpost.

St. Francis Mission was actually under construction when they arrived. The Jesuit Fathers and the Sisters of St. Francis greeted the guests with a joyous welcome. Apparently they did not know that there would be women in the party so it was necessary to provide makeshift sleeping accommodations for them. There were no curtains for the windows. The sisters awoke the next morning to see a group of Sioux peering in at the strange visitors from the big city out east.

It was on behalf of this mission in Rosebud that the priests visited Katharine and as a result of her personal generosity they not only continued the mission itself but were also building a new school and convent.

They attended morning Mass at seven and followed the service with a huge feast. The sisters were fascinated in their tour of the village and they saw the beautiful, bright colored shawls worn by the women and the brightly painted faces of the men. The Sioux were also fascinated with the trinkets and dolls their guests had brought with them from Omaha. It was the first of many learning experiences that Katharine shared with her new Native American friends.

Next they visited the Holy Rosary Mission and the home of the legendary Chief Red Cloud. They gave the chief and his wife gifts, but he told the visitors that the new school built for his people was the greatest gift of all. Next they visited the Immaculate Conception Mission. The buildings were constructed entirely from funds provided by Katharine. She named the mission after her mother Emma's favorite title of the

Virgin. It was here that the sisters were for the first time truly frightened. It happened when they were invited to join Father Stephan at a tribal war dance. Sister Dolores in her book on the Drexel family described what happened.

She tells us that the Sioux were dressed in war paint, a few feathers and bells on their knees. Their music was wild and they danced in a frenzy. The sisters became very uncomfortable with the performance. Katharine took Elizabeth aside and whispered to her, "This is awful. What shall we do? Shall we go or stay?"

"Let's watch the sisters," answered Elizabeth, "If they stick it out, we will have to stay."

The sisters stayed. But Father Stephan had a very sore foot and suddenly got up and limped away. Elizabeth, Katharine and Louise quickly got up and followed him out.

The visitors stopped at several other stations. They traveled by train and by wagon. From the town of Rugby they traveled by train to St. Paul where they stayed at a real hotel for the first time in weeks. There they met Archbishop John Ireland who told them he was not optimistic about the missions. Leaving the archbishop, Elizabeth remarked, "He is in some ways a gloomy prognosticator, but he is an excellent host."

The next summer the three sisters accepted an invitation to visit more of the missions. This time they journeyed to the northern reservations in Wisconsin and Minnesota. These foundations were all the recipients of Drexel family generosity. The highlight of this trip occurred in Red Lake. After Mass one morning, several baptisms were celebrated. Katharine was surprised when one of the mothers asked her to be the godmother for her son William. Throughout her life she prayed often for her spiritual son and his family.

On the family, but especially on Katharine, these trips to visit the various missionary establishments made a deep impression.

Surely as she witnessed first hand the success of the work of the missionary priests and sisters, she must have pondered over and over the question asked of her by Pope Leo XIII. Most certainly she wanted to answer the call of the Holy Father. Despite her desire to dedicate her life to the Church, she had nagging doubts about her worthiness and her readiness. She turned to her spiritual father for his insight and advice.

She had long since made Bishop O'Connor aware of the pope's suggestion. He seemed to be torn between two possible paths she could follow. He explained that she could either establish a new missionary congregation or she could join a group that was already experienced in this type of religious vocation among the Native Americans. Apparently he tried to help her to make this important decision by sending her to visit a group of missions so that she could come face-to-face with the work of religious missionaries.

Both realized that it was not just the lack of funds that stood in the way of progress. Far more important was the lack of permanent staff to work on the reservations. Some religious congregations agreed to staff a mission but only for a limited time. When the period of service ended, the whole group went home. It was difficult, if not impossible, to obtain replacements.

After her visits to the field, Katharine was convinced there was a great need for a religious congregation that would work solely with Native Americans. She was also now sure that her own religious vocation did not involve a contemplative order. She knew now that she should and would work to improve the lot of Native Americans.

She still was not convinced that she should do this work within an existing religious order. However, when speaking with Bishop O'Connor, with her Jesuit confessor in Philadelphia, Father E. J. McGoldrick, and with her sisters, she often said that she believed she lacked the ability to found and then to direct a new religious order.

After serious prayer and a novena to the Holy Spirit, she decided that the only place that she could turn to discern the will of God was to her spiritual father, the Bishop of Omaha. While she was planning how to go about this, her "little sister" Louise came to her with the news that she planned to get married.

Since the death of their father, the three Drexel sisters had become very close. They lived as a family. Part of the year they lived in the town house in the city and the remainder of the year in their country home at Torresdale. They went to Europe and visited the missions in the west together. If they were separated even for a few days, they kept in touch by mail.

This closeness was illustrated in a letter Katharine wrote to her sisters while visiting their uncle in New York City. She wrote them these endearing words: "If my heart does not belong to you, my sisters, to whom does it belong? It is useless to say once again that I am always lovingly a part of yourselves—one of the All Three." In their correspondence they often referred to themselves by that title, "The All Three."

In January of 1889, Louise married Colonel Edward Morell. He was a very prominent, rising young lawyer whose wealthy family was involved in the social life of Philadelphia. Fortunately, he was a devout Catholic who was deeply concerned about the needs of the city's poor community. He supported the sisters in their efforts on behalf of the missions and truly became one of the family.

It was a huge wedding involving two of the city's most socially prominent Catholic families. The Archbishop himself presided at the solemn Mass. Bishop O'Connor celebrated the Nuptial Mass and was assisted by Father Stephan and other priest friends of the families. Uncle Anthony Drexel gave the bride away and Katharine served as maid of honor for her sister. In a remarkable series of events "The All Three" suddenly all went their separate ways. Although they remained very close, their lives radically changed. Louise married in January 1889; Katharine entered the convent in May of 1889 and Elizabeth was married to Walter G. Smith in January of 1890. In less than a year, all three sisters left the Walnut Street homestead to begin new lives.

# CHAPTER 7

## SAYING YES TO THE LORD

Who would have guessed that the beautiful young woman who served as maid of honor at the fashionable wedding of Louise Drexel would in a few short months be beginning her training for the religious life in a Pittsburgh convent. Dancing with the best man she gave no outward indication of the fact that she was ready to dedicate her life to the Lord in the service of her less fortunate brothers and sisters. Her sisters, her family and her close friends knew some of the turmoil she was undergoing in finally trying to decide whether or not the Lord was calling her to the life of a missionary sister.

Shortly after her return from her last European trip, Katharine came to the decision that she had a religious vocation. For almost two years she struggled with the form that vocation would take. Her spiritual directors, Bishop O'Connor in Omaha and Father McGoldrick in Philadelphia, through letters and personal conversations, tried to guide her to a better understanding of what the Lord had in mind for her.

At the start, Father McGoldrick, a Jesuit priest, suggested the method of St. Ignatius to determine a course of action. He asked her to list the reasons for or against the missionary religious vocation. She sent the results of this procedure to the bishop. This began a series of correspondence on the subject that lasted until the day she entered the convent six years later.

In these letters Katharine tried to explain her feelings, to describe her prayer life, and to share her deep interest in helping the poverty stricken Native Americans.

At first Bishop O'Connor believed that she could accomplish what she sought and remain in the world giving good example to other women of means. He suggested that she take an annual vow of virginity that could be renewed indefinitely. After several letters, they abandoned this course of action and Katharine was encouraged to simplify her lifestyle and to attempt to adopt the prayer life of a religious.

Later the bishop was concerned about her ability to live the life of a religious considering her health problems. She spent several weeks eating the rations that were the ordinary diet of active religious at that time. This convinced them that she would be able to function under these circumstances. Actually she would live the difficult life of a missionary religious sister for 66 years and die at the age of 97.

After a series of many letters, Bishop O'Connor decided quite suddenly that there were no obstacles remaining in the way of her entering the religious life. On November 30, 1888, he gave his approval with these words, "I have come to regard it as certain that Our Lord has chosen you for Himself, but, for reasons with which you are familiar, I was inclined to think He wished you to love and serve Him not as His spouse, but in society. This letter of yours, and your bearing under the long and severe tests to which I subjected you, as well as your entire restoration to health, and the many spiritual dangers that surround you, make me withdraw all opposition to your entering religion."

The bishop went on to say that the decision now was which congregation would she join. He gave her three possibilities. She hesitated choosing any one of them because she wanted to receive Holy Communion every day. Daily Communion was allowed in most of the contemplative orders but missionary orders usually had no provision for daily Communion. This was very important to her and she would not consider the congregation that did not provide for daily Communion. She also made it clear to the bishop that "I want a missionary order for Indians and Colored People."

While pondering her own future as a religious she was truly concerned that the needs of poor blacks and Native Americans be cared for. She wanted to enter the convent quickly but she also wanted to make sure that the money that was needed would be available in her trust fund. When this was found to be the case, another obstacle fell by the wayside.

Katharine continued to argue that she was not able to found a new community and be its superior. She had little confidence in her own leadership ability. She listed for her spiritual adviser a series of objections. He rejected them all and wrote her, "The more I have thought of your case, the more convinced I become that God has called you to establish an order for the Indians and Negroes."

He then enlisted the aid of Archbishop Ireland. The archbishop replied, "It is just the thing we need. It's a great and indispensable work. Miss Drexel is just the person to do it."

Katharine finally gave in to the advice of her clerical friends. She agreed that on May 7 she would enter the Sisters of Mercy Convent in Pittsburgh. There she would begin her training in the religious life. It was decided that she should have a two-year period of preparation and would be treated like the other postulants to the order.

Not all approved of Katharine's decision. Some of the trustees of her father's estate were shocked. Uncle Anthony had tears in his eyes and begged her to change her mind saying, "It is little short of a tragedy for you to do this. Stay with us who love you." Uncle George Childs said it was a foolish thing to do and actually went to Archbishop Ryan asking him to try to prevent her from entering. Both of her uncles knew it was hopeless and reluctantly gave their blessing.

Accompanied by her two sisters, Mary Cassidy and Johanna Ryan, she presented herself to the superior, Sister Sebastian Gillespie, and began a 66 year career as a religious missionary.

Her sisters left the new postulant. Louise and her new husband were to leave for Europe the next day. Elizabeth, not wanting to be alone at St. Michael's, joined them on their trip to the continent. Mother Sebastian promised them that Katharine could mail and receive letters as often as she wanted.

Shortly after they left, the new postulant was taken to the convent parlor and welcomed into the community. She was given her new postulant's dress and called upon to read the prayers at the first chapel session she attended.

Her entrance into the convent was noted in newspapers throughout the country. At the convent, the Sisters of Mercy made every effort to treat the new member just like any other postulant. In the middle of that first morning they had to send away a newspaper reporter who came to seek an interview.

The first few months passed swiftly as Sister Katharine quickly adjusted to convent life. Even the "convent rations" seemed to please her. She always insisted on being treated exactly like all the rest and was very upset to find that she was the only sister to receive an orange at breakfast. She insisted that the practice stop. It was when her six months as a postulant were coming to a close before most of the convent knew that she was going to found her own congregation. As she prepared to enter the novitiate in November, at the suggestion of the superior, she chose to use her own name in the religious life. She was to be called Sister Katharine in honor of her patron St. Catherine of Siena.

There was a great celebration at St. Mary's Convent in Pittsburgh on November 7. On that day Katharine Drexel was received as a novice. Since she was still in control of her family inheritance, she made arrangements for her one last personal expenditure. She chartered a private railroad car to bring her family and friends from Philadelphia to the ceremony. All— from the young cousins to Uncle Anthony and Uncle George— almost filled the convent chapel.

Archbishop Ryan presided at the ceremony and blessed the simple black habit of a novice. As Sister Katharine knelt before him, the archbishop blessed her and received her promises as a novice. He then gave a brief sermon in which he said that Katharine was not entering a life of serenity, but that she was to live a life of service on behalf of God's poor.

At the end of the moving service, as Sister Katharine stood before him, the archbishop spoke these prophetic words directly to the new novice:

> "In His Name, I invite you into this sanctuary.
> Thousands of Indians and the colored races unite
> their voices with mine in crying out to you,
> Come, we have waited for you. God is
> sending you. Come!"

Following the ceremonies, the three sisters had some time to themselves. Happiness was on their faces. Then Sister Katharine paused and voiced her concern that from now on Elizabeth would be alone in St. Michael's. She feared that she would live a lonely life. Suddenly Elizabeth announced, "Don't worry dear, I am going to marry Walter George Smith in January and we want to buy St. Michael's as our future home."

Before they left the convent, Sister asked her two sisters to try to find some land around Torresdale where they could build a motherhouse for the new congregation. A short time later, Louise wrote that she had found the perfect spot in Cornwells Heights, just a few miles from St. Michael's. The family promised to set the property aside until the new foundress could come to look it over.

Time continued to pass swiftly and soon Sister Katharine was spending her first Christmas separated from her sisters and her family. The All-Three were still united especially in their many acts of charity made possible as a result of their father's trust fund. Their common interests kept them in close contact by mail as the preparation continued for Elizabeth's wedding on January 7. Archbishop Ryan and all the family friends celebrated the great day. During the ceremony, the arch-bishop spoke of "the novice in a distant convent praying for her loved ones."

During the summer months Bishop O'Connor's health had begun to fail. In the late fall his doctor told him he could not endure the cold winters in the northwest country and insisted he spend some time in the South. He journeyed to Mississippi and Alabama and was soon interested in the plight of the poor blacks of the South. His health was not restored and he wrote back that he felt crushed and forsaken. Mother Sebastian decid-ed that she and Sister Katharine should go down to Alabama and bring the sick bishop to Mercy Hospital in Pittsburgh. Here he would be close to the sisters and to his brother, Michael O'Connor, the bishop of Pittsburgh.

With good care from the hospital sisters, the sick bishop made somewhat of a recovery. He knew, however, that the end was near and asked to be brought back to end his life among his people in Nebraska. He died in his Episcopal residence on May 27, 1890.

His passing was a real blow to the new novice. She told her family that his death was almost as great a loss as the death of her parents. In many ways the bishop had taken the place of her much loved mother and father. He had been with her in times of crisis and decision. During her months in the convent he had been an enormous tower of strength. His absence from her life would create a great void that made her fear for the future of her vocation. She wondered where she would get the courage to begin her new foundation.

Archbishop Ryan went to Omaha to celebrate the Requiem Mass for his good friend and then on his way home he stopped to console a grieving Sister Katharine. She told the prelate that she could not go on alone. She seriously doubted her ability as a religious superior, and that perhaps she could do more good for the Native Americans and blacks if she lived in the world.

The compassionate archbishop looked into her tear-filled face and offered his help with these kind words, "We have both lost a good friend whose heart was gentle. But now please tell me, will it help you if I promise to be your father-in-Christ and share the burden with you so that you can come to me when you need help? Then do you think you can stay?"

The color returned to her face. The tears dried and she was full of hope again. She knelt to kiss the archbishop's ring and said with a strong voice, "I will stay, your grace."

Since his coming to Philadelphia, Archbishop Ryan had been a friend of the Drexel family. He joined them on their joyful and sorrowful celebrations. It was fitting that he serve as spiritual mentor for Katharine as she prepared to begin such a huge undertaking as the foundation of a new religious congregation. His advice and counsel would be invaluable in the months ahead as she broke new ground and became a pioneer in the field of social justice at the start of the 20th century. He was for her a pillar of strength.

The summer passed quickly and in the first week of September Elizabeth and her husband returned from their European honeymoon. She was expecting her first child in December and asked the sisters in Mercy Convent to make a layette for the expected baby. She was delighted to hear that Sister Katharine and her nuns had begun the construction of the new motherhouse near Torresdale. After a long separation she was delighted that the All-Three would soon be closer together again.

Elizabeth and Walter Smith arrived home on September 7. The pregnant wife was not feeling well. She had the flu before getting on the ship and by the time they reached Philadelphia she was very ill. The baby was born prematurely. Both child and mother died.

Sister Katharine was given permission to attend the funeral. The burial took place at St. Michael's in the same oratory in which all of the Drexel girls had received their First Holy Communion. She knelt before the tomb, crushed by the recent deaths of her father, mother, Bishop O'Connor and now sister and infant niece. It was with a heavy heart that she returned to the convent in Pittsburgh to continue her preparations for the foundation of her missionary order.

True to his word, the archbishop was always at her side ready to help. In late November he, along with Cardinal James Gibbons, the archbishop of Baltimore, came to visit the new community. The cardinal was impressed with their progress and with the leadership demonstrated by the new foundress. In a small gathering in the convent chapel, the cardinal blessed them and told them that "Your work is a truly apostolic one. Be apostles and carry the glad tidings of the Gospel to those neglected races, for 'beautiful are the feet that carry the gospel to heathen lands.' "

The foundress always remembered the cardinal's words and referred to herself and the band of sisters as apostles for social justice in the world.

During those days of transition, the foundress had many important duties. Not only did she have the task of preparing the first members of the Sisters of the Blessed Sacrament in their mission activities, but she was called upon to distribute financial help to those who sought her aid. Much of her time was spent trying to satisfy the most desperate calls for financial assistance. She and Father Stephan were greatly concerned about the ending of the Contract System for the Mission schools. The burden of operating these schools fell on the various religious congregations and they came to the Drexel family trust fund for help.

During the period of novitiate, Sister Katharine had contributed more than $50,000 to work among the Native Americans, and through her help seven new mission outposts were set up in the West and Southwest. Although most of her income and her efforts were on behalf of Native Americans, she was becoming more and more aware of and responsive to the need of poor blacks especially in the South. More and more she was determined that a ministry to blacks be an important part of the congregation she was to found.

As the period of her novitiate was drawing to a close, she consulted with Archbishop Ryan on two important questions. First, they were to agree upon a name for the new congregation, and then they were to decide on the location for the new motherhouse. Sister Katharine chose the name "Sisters of the Blessed Sacrament." Bishop O'Connor had given approval. When the time drew near, she asked her new spiritual father what his thoughts were. He liked the name but strongly suggested that the words "for Indians and Negroes" be added. The foundress thought it was an excellent idea and the congregation was so named.

Many different proposals were made as to the place where the new motherhouse should be built. Father Stephan suggested Bannong, California because it was close to many reservations. Bishop Marty offered to help with the construction of the motherhouse in Sioux Falls, South Dakota. Members of the Drexel family felt that the new building should be near Philadelphia and selected a piece of property near Torresdale in Cornwells Heights. The archbishop thought it would be a good idea for the sisters' headquarters to be built in his archdiocese. The foundress agreed and it was settled.

Other decisions were made about the vows that were to be taken, the habit that was to be worn, and the place where the novitiate would be held. Then all was in readiness for the great day when Sister Mary Katharine Drexel was to make her profession as the first sister of the Sisters of the Blessed Sacrament for Indians and Colored People. It was on February 12, 1891 that she became the foundress of a new missionary congregation.

First Profession in Pittsburgh parlor of the Sisters of Mercy Convent.

73

# CHAPTER 8

# THE FOUNDATION OF A CONGREGATION

"I do vow and promise to God, for five years from this date, poverty, chastity and obedience, and to be a mother and servant of the Indians and the colored people; nor shall I undertake any work which may lead to the neglect or abandonment of the Indians and the colored races." With these words the Sisters of the Blessed Sacrament for Indians and Negroes came into being. After Sister Mary Katharine signed the parchment placed into her hands by Archbishop Ryan, he appointed her superior and she became Mother Katharine Drexel.

It was a simple but historic ceremony. It would have a profound effect upon the history of race relations in our country for decades to come. The woman who stood before the altar and made her religious profession would one day be canonized a saint for her life of heroic virtue.

Four years before in Rome the Holy Father, Pope Leo III, asked her a question," Why not be a missionary yourself, my child?" On the afternoon of her profession, Mother Katharine received a telegram from the Vatican which read: "Holy Father's blessing on your profession and charities."

There were only a few present to celebrate with her. Gathered in the small chapel were Mother Katharine and the ten novices of the new community, the Sisters of Mercy, Archbishop Ryan, Bishop Richard Phelan of Pittsburgh, Bishop Marty and Monsignor Stephan. Louise, still mourning the sudden death of their sister Elizabeth, was unable to make the trip. The new superior had no desire that there be a large congregation and was delighted with the presence of her closest relatives and friends and her new community.

Archbishop Ryan, who was anxious to get the community settled in his archdiocese, decided that until the new motherhouse was completed the novitiate would be housed in the Drexel summer house at Torresdale. The new superior was delighted with the choice and began to make arrangements for the move. It was a comfortable place for the novices to live. Empty now since the death of Elizabeth, its beautiful chapel and grounds provided a fitting place for prayer and meditation.

The archbishop set July 1 as the opening day for the novitiate. The new superior spent the next few months transforming the summer home of a wealthy banker into a convent that would house a group of young women aspiring to the religious life. The immediate plans were to take in some black homeless children from the inner city. The work on a place for them to stay, called Holy Family Mission, began at once.

As soon as some makeshift quarters could be arranged, the superior left Pittsburgh with four novices and one postulant and a ten-year-old girl who was to be the first black child to live in the new mission. For the first few nights, they all stayed in one room. Soon a cottage was provided for some children to come from Pittsburgh and Philadelphia. These were the members of the first foundation set up by the newly formed Sisters of the Blessed Sacrament. The homeless children got a place to stay in the country and the new sisters got some practical experience for their future work with young people.

Two valuable additions to the staff helped the new congregation to build a foundation in the spiritual life. From Pittsburgh, the Sisters of Mercy sent Mother Mary Inez, a veteran spiritual director, who would become the first mistress of novices. Father John Scull, a Jesuit priest from Philadelphia, came once a month for conferences, spiritual direction and to serve as confessor. Both of these spiritual leaders made an enormous contribution during that first year for that new religious community.

Before the group was able to settle down, their first distinguished visitor was Archbishop Francis Janssens of New Orleans. He was very concerned about the poor black children in his care. His archdiocese was in severe financial difficulty and he had nowhere to turn. The archbishop and the foundress became great friends and marked the beginning of a long relationship between the congregation and the archdiocese. The New Orleans area was to become a special apostolate for Mother Katharine and the scene of one of her greatest achievements—Xavier University. In June, Archbishop Ryan arrived to inspect the new novitiate. He celebrated the Eucharist in the hall and reception room in the Drexel family country house. The area had been converted into the new convent chapel. He blessed the new facilities and placed the Eucharist in a makeshift tabernacle that was to be the center of worship for the members of the Sisters of the Blessed Sacrament. The Eucharist was reserved in their home, but it would be some time before the foundress could arrange for the celebration of daily Mass. This was for her a primary consideration.

During those first days the superior received an urgent letter of invitation from Bishop Maurice F. Burke of Cheyenne. The letter concerned St. Stephen Mission in Wyoming. This was one of the projects of her friend Bishop O'Connor. She had financed the construction of a school that had no teachers. The Jesuit Mission was asking help from the new congregation. Bishop Burke asked the superior to come out to the mission in order to understand their difficult situation.

Mother Katharine, accompanied by Sister Patrick, made the first of what would be many trips to missionary fields in an effort to determine how her sisters could help. It was a long and difficult trip on an old stagecoach. When they got to the school, they found out that the lay faculty had left because there were no funds to pay them. The children were there with no one to teach them.

The superior was truly moved by the sight and promised Bishop Burke to do whatever she could. In her own mind she thought of St. Stephen's as her congregation's first foundation. She planned to try to get sisters to go to Wyoming in August. She even arranged for furniture and equipment to be sent on when the sisters were ready to go. Bishop Burke was delighted at the prospect.

When she got back to Philadelphia, she immediately went to see the archbishop. It was her first disappointment in the religious life. Archbishop Ryan refused to give the community permission to take on the mission. He told Mother Katharine that her sisters, many of whom had been in the religious life for less than a year, simply did not have the necessary experience. The difficult life in the primitive Wyoming countryside would prove to be too much of a sudden change for the young women from Philadelphia and Pittsburgh. They needed more time to grow in the spiritual life and in teaching experience.

Disappointed though she was, the new foundress realized in her heart that the wise archbishop was right. She did not abandon Bishop Burke's mission, but traveled to Kansas and convinced the Sisters of St. Joseph they should staff the mission on a temporary basis. Bishop Burke was delighted with the arrangement, knowing that he would have a strong ally in his future efforts to expand his missionary activities.

Mother Katharine resumed her plan to provide her new sisters with serious spiritual training and a knowledge of the workings of community. Mother Mary Inez proved to be a fantastic asset. A veteran mistress of novices, she quickly attained the respect and admiration of the fledgling community. There were some problems, however, because none of the novices were efficient at household chores. Their overeagerness to help out sometimes caused more problems. On one occasion when Archbishop Janssens was visiting from New Orleans and having quiet conversation with Mother Inez, suddenly a huge crash was heard coming from the kitchen. Unruffled, the archbishop said, "You know, mother, it is said that the worth of a vocation is not determined by the number of things a postulant breaks."

Mother Inez answered with a smile, "Then everyone here must have a true vocation."

Plans for the new motherhouse were well under way. It was to be located in Cornwells Heights in the town of Bensalem, Bucks County, Pennsylvania. For 110 years it has been the center of activity for the Sisters of the Blessed Sacrament. From there sisters were sent out from one end of the country to the other. It still stands today and has become a site for pilgrimages to honor Mother Katharine and her faithful missionaries.

July 16, 1891 was the date chosen for the laying of the cornerstone for the new structure. It was also the day on which the whole community for the first time put on the official habit of the new congregation. It was a moving ceremony. Mr. and Mrs. Morrell provided carriages to transport all of the sisters to the motherhouse site. With prophetic wisdom, the foundress had written on the new cornerstone these words of the Apostle Paul: "It shall be the place where it is said to them: You are not my people; there they shall be called the sons of the living God."

The spiritual father of the community, Archbishop Ryan, assisted by Father Lawrence Wall, presided over the blessing ceremony. The clergy also officiated at the groundbreaking ceremonies for the new Holy Providence Institute for black children, located on the grounds of the motherhouse.

Following the ceremonies the sisters and their guests gathered together for refreshments. The Sisters of the Blessed Sacrament had taken a giant step forward.

While the ceremony was being carried out, there were more than a dozen plain clothesmen on watch. They were hired by the archbishop to protect the sisters and guests from serious physical harm. Remarkable as it may seem in 1891, that cornerstone blessing was the scene of a bomb scare. All who participated were in danger by the threatening action of a handful of disgruntled neighbors.

The afternoon before the ceremony a large stick of dynamite was found at the place marked out for the cornerstone. Rumors spread throughout the community that the local farmers were not interested in having a convent of Catholic sisters and a school for Negro children being built in the midst of their farm land. One of the leaders of the group apparently threatened that all of the Catholics who would be sitting on the platform would be blown to hell in the midst of the ceremony.

To confound the would-be terrorists, the architect constructed on the cornerstone site a large wooden box that was nailed shut. He posted a large sign with the words: "Hands Off - High Explosives." An armed guard stood by next to the box all day. The guard ordered everyone not to come near or the vibration might cause an explosion. The plan worked out well—not a single farmer came near the box. Archbishop Ryan hid the story of the dynamite from the community. It was many years later, according to the congregation archives, that the superior and sisters found out about the dangerous situation.

During her more than sixty years as superior, Mother Mary Katharine would supervise the construction of many buildings that would be used to spread the Word of God to those who were committed to her care. These buildings would be used to provide an education for countless thousands of Native Americans and blacks. They would also provide a clean and safe place in which they could grow up to become productive citizens of our land. In the course of the long years of her religious life, hatred and bigotry would continue to block her efforts on behalf of human rights. Unafraid, she never allowed it to stand in the way of the cause of social justice for her Native American and black brothers and sisters.

It is hard to believe that the building in which her apostolate was to start would somehow become a target for destruction before her work had even begun. Being an apostle of social justice at the start of the 20th century would prove to be no easy task.

As the novices continued to grow in the spiritual life, Mother Inez was called home to Pittsburgh. The new foundress was greatly disappointed. She had come to depend upon her wise guidance. Mother Inez tried to reassure her and said, "It is best that I go. You are a far better Mistress of Novices than I would ever be."

In September the new congregation held their first reception and profession ceremonies. Of course, faithful Archbishop Ryan presided at the profession and would continue to do so until the year he died.

A steady stream of ecclesiastical dignitaries visited Mother Katharine during the months in which the new motherhouse was being constructed. Bishops from New Orleans, the Oklahoma territory, North Carolina and Cheyenne came to the new community seeking help. They spoke to the nuns and described their missionary work. It was a great learning experience for the novices.

One of these meetings, however, did not work out as planned. Even potential saints make an occasional mistake of judgment. The superior invited an impressive Native American missionary to speak to the sisters one Sunday. He told them that he was unworthy to address them but he would give his blessing. His piety greatly impressed the inexperienced sisters. The superior was so impressed that she gave him $10 to purchase some vestments. A few months later word came back that he was a bogus priest who was collecting funds for a missionary group that did not exist.

The new motherhouse was scheduled to open in June of 1892. A serious cave-in delayed the work for weeks. The weight of huge Spanish tiles on the roof of the chapel almost caused the walls to collapse. The architect was called and special buttresses were installed to insure the safety of the building. The superior was greatly upset by the delays and announced in September that the sisters would move into the new building on December 3, the feast of St. Francis Xavier. She announced that the new sisters would occupy their new home on that feast day—ready or not. It was not really ready but they moved in nonetheless.

On their arrival, they lacked a few amenities. There was no heat. There were no lights. There was no water. Despite these inconveniences, they were delighted to take up residence in their beautiful new building. The fifteen orphan children who had lived with them in St. Michael's came with them and moved into the Holy Providence School, which was likewise still under construction.

When the sisters arrived the place was wide open. There were no locks on the doors or curtains on the windows. There was a completed area where the sisters could live in safety and by February the new school for homeless children was completed. It was immediately occupied to its capacity. Since then the school has been enlarged to several times its original size.

Archbishop Ryan, the sisters and the Drexel family were all delighted with the new quarters. Demands for help continued to pour in especially from the midwest and south. The archbishop insisted that the new congregation was not prepared to undertake any missionary apostolate at this time. He required that the new sisters undergo a period of training in both spirituality and missionary training. He thought—to the disappointment of the sisters—that this training would take several more years.

By mid-January, the Sisters of the Blessed Sacrament had settled down in their new headquarters. It was a large building for its day. The new chapel comfortably seated sixty sisters. At the end of the month a profession of vows took place in the new chapel. They did not fill the sixty stalls; but what they lacked in numbers, they made up for in enthusiasm. The archbishop remarked to them at the reception that they were, indeed, few in numbers but they were destined to lead many others to Jesus by their example and their teaching. How right he was!

It was at this time that the new superior received word of the death of her uncle, Anthony Drexel. He had been ailing for some time but seemed to be improving. His passing was quite unexpected and the Drexel sisters were overwhelmed with grief. Since the death of their own father, Katharine and Louise had learned to depend upon the wisdom and direction of their lovable uncle. He was their last strong male role model from their parents' generation. The passing of Anthony Drexel was marked with a huge memorial service held at the Drexel Institute. All of the religious, political and financial leaders of the Philadelphia community mourned his passing. For Katharine and Louise his passing marked the end of an era.

In the next few months the new congregation developed a routine that included spiritual direction, work with the children in the boarding school, and learning from experienced missionaries that came to help prepare the sisters.

Two missionary bishops visited the new motherhouse in 1883. They came on behalf of St. Catherine School in Santa Fe, New Mexico. Seven years before the Drexel family had given the school the money to construct the building. Under the direction of the archbishop, about seventy Native American boys had been brought there for religious instruction and training for life in the world. The Sisters of Loretto conducted the school for several years and they were replaced by a lay director and two lay women. After a year the lay faculty left, complaining that the work was too demanding and the place was a lonely outpost.

Archbishop P. L. Chapelle, the archbishop of Santa Fe, pleaded with the congregation to help before the children were lost and the building lay in ruin.

Mother Katharine went to her spiritual father to plead the case. This time he did not refuse. Archbishop Ryan asked that the sisters delay their mission in Santa Fe for a year. When he found out that St. Catherine's School had already been closed, he gave the Sisters of the Blessed Sacrament permission to take over the mission as soon as possible, and to try to bring back to that Catholic school those orphans who were being deprived of a religious education.

The sisters were delighted. The new congregation began its first mission. Mother Katharine was on the train to Santa Fe. The Sisters of the Blessed Sacrament were about to begin the work for which the congregation was founded.

Mother Katharine

# CHAPTER 9

# FIRST MISSION:
# ST. CATHERINE'S SCHOOL

As their train pulled into the railroad station at Lamy, the Mother Superior and her companion, Sister Mary Evangelist, looked out the window to the platform. Standing there they saw Archbishop Chapelle with his arms outstretched. As the nuns left the train, he rushed over to them and shouted, "Thank God, thank God, my prayer has been answered. You are coming to take care of St. Catherine's School."

The archbishop's enthusiastic welcome was most sincere. When the two sisters had the opportunity to see the school and the area and to meet with some of the people involved, they quickly shared his enthusiasm. They found the facilities in excellent condition. In most cases all that would have to be done was a job of clean-up. They found parents who were most willing to send their children to learn about the White Man's God.

When Archbishop Ryan heard the glowing reports of the situation at St. Catherine's, he too was caught up in the prospect of the first missionary effort of the new Sisters of the Blessed Sacrament. From the time the superior returned with her glowing report, he never once hesitated about the starting time and never once expressed the notion that the new, untrained sisters needed more time for preparation.

After consultation with the archbishop, it was decided that the school would be open to girls as well as boys. Very quickly it was apparent that there would be far more seeking admission than could be accommodated by the new facility.

Some would be disappointed at least for the first year of operation.

After much soul searching Mother Katharine decided that the most she could possibly send was a total of nine sisters. Just about everyone in the congregation wanted to go. When the selection was made, there were many left disappointed. In the spirit of community they came together to help those who were selected to make the first missionary trip.

Mother Evangelist was appointed the first superior of the new mission group and Archbishop Ryan was on hand when the first four sisters left for Santa Fe. He offered his prayers and a blessing and the tears flowed freely. All present were well aware that it was an historic moment in the history of the fledgling congregation.

Mother Katharine, her ever present diary in hand, marked the date—June 18, 1894. It was the first of a long series of departure services at the motherhouse. In the years to come hundreds of sisters would leave St. Elizabeth Convent to go out to the four corners of the country to spread the message of Jesus Christ.

After the tears of departure, it was a glorious trip. The excited sisters were met and brought to their new school with a warm New Mexico welcome. They immediately went to work.

With the second group of five sisters that left the following week, it was an entirely different story. As soon as they reached the train station in Chicago, the whole western train system was shut down. They found themselves in the midst of the 1894 Pullman strike which had taken a violent turn. Twice the sisters were abandoned as strikers ran away with the engines leaving scores of passengers stuck in the railroad cars in the middle of the desert. The discouraged sisters telegraphed the motherhouse for directions. The superior replied that if there was any danger to the sisters safety, they should not try to continue the journey.

The president ordered the United States Army to see to it that the trains got through. The sisters boarded the train in Colorado and had a wild ride through treacherous weather. A portion of the final leg of the long and much delayed trip was made in freight cars.

The exhausted sisters finally arrived at the mission and were welcomed by the four members of the community who had already settled down. The next few weeks were busy ones as the missionaries prepared the school and facilities for the opening of the fall term in September. Looking back at the dangerous and difficult trip to their first mission, the superior often told her sisters that the Lord used this experience to let them know that the life of a missionary would not be an easy one.

Mother Katharine was concerned about the welfare of her sisters so far away from the rest of the community. The mail service was painfully slow and there were long periods in which no mail was received. Always concerned about those in her charge, she decided to make the difficult trip to New Mexico to learn just how things were going at the opening of school.

She arrived by hack from Lamy very late at night. The mission was in darkness and all the doors carefully locked. Fortunately, the hack driver had a match and found the Angelus bell. The tired superior gave the rope a hard pull. The sound of the bell woke up the whole community. "Sisters, it is Mother Katharine," she cried out. With that all nine sisters rushed downstairs to give the superior a warm welcome to St. Catherine's School.

The next few days were a flurry of excitement. Mother superior found that the enrollment was not what she expected. A quick visit to Bishop Chapelle assured her that the children would be there opening day. She met with them and through an interpreter, spoke to the parents of the children. On opening day there were tears of happiness on the part of parents and teachers alike. All were delighted and Katharine made the long trip back to the motherhouse with a happy heart.

The new year, 1895, began with happy moments. On January 9, Archbishop Ryan came to celebrate the Eucharist and to hear the foundress' solemn vows. For the first time all the stalls in the motherhouse chapel were filled to capacity. Relatives and friends were on hand. The almost 200 children in the Holy Providence Mission were part of the celebration. With this ceremony began the custom of giving each sister who made her vows a silver ring that was to be a symbol of their perpetual espousal.

In a ceremony that has become a tradition with the Sisters of the Blessed Sacrament, the archbishop said to her, "Wear the ring of faith, the seal of the Holy Ghost." In response, Mother Katharine replied: "I am espoused to Him whom the angels serve."

A few months later, in mid May, the superior decided that she would drop in at St. Catherine's as the school year was drawing to a close. She surprised the faculty who were over-joyed to see her. She was pleased to see what had been accomplished in the first year at the Santa Fe school. Everything was running smoothly. The school was filled to capacity. The bishop was delighted with the progress.

There was a sense of peace and joy among the faculty, the students and their parents. To help lighten the heavy teaching burden, the superior brought along two additional sisters to help with the teaching responsibilities. She congratulated Mother Mary Evangelist and her staff on the job they were doing and they discussed expanding the program.

Mother Katharine was preparing to return to Philadelphia, when the sisters learned of a horrible plague that was raging in the San Domingo Pueblo. A large number of men, women and children were deathly ill and there were very few available to care for them. The government sent doctors and nurses to help and many of them were so inexperienced working with the contagion, they too were inflicted with the deadly symptoms.

Delaying her trip home, the foundress decided something drastic must be done on behalf of the victims. She sent word to her spiritual father that she and Mother Evangelist were going to San Domingo to nurse those who had been afflicted by the plague. She told her sisters at St. Catherine's that they were going and instructed them not to tell the sisters in the motherhouse who would be upset to hear the fearful news.

There was nothing the sisters could do to persuade their superiors that it was too dangerous to go alone. Supplies of medicines and food were gathered and the two determined mothers started out in a horse and wagon to the plague infested pueblo.

The sisters back at St. Catherine's gathered the children in prayer. The safety of the two volunteer nurses was uppermost in their minds. All day the community was united in a common effort. Hundreds of rosaries were recited praying for the safe return of their beloved superior and her companion. They contacted Archbishop Ryan and informed him what had happened. He was told by the authorities that there were a sufficient number of doctors and nurses on hand to take care of the plague victims.

When it was reported that several of the early caregivers who had not taken precautions to avoid being contaminated had fallen victim to the plague, he tried in vain to contact the sisters. The prayers of all involved were answered in a strange way. When Mother Katharine and her companion reached San Domingo, they were exhausted from the long journey. Finally they reached the pueblo only to have the Council of the Pueblo deny their entrance until they had assembled and decided how to react to this outside help.

The would-be nurses waited a whole day for the decision. As the sisters waited at the entrance, the governor of the pueblo came out to see them. He told them that under no circumstances could they even visit or see the sick. In her memoirs Mother Mercedes reports that the governor made his decision very clear when he told the sisters, "You go back to church and pray for them."

The governor's word was final. The two mothers were welcomed back to St. Catherine's with a big celebration. The sisters and children were delighted to have them back safe and sound. Mother Mercedes, who had remained home, was happy to report to the community that the nurse volunteers did not even get the opportunity to open their trunks of medicines and supplies.

In the spring of 1896, Mother Katharine returned to Santa Fe and had a long visitation at the mission. She grew to have a special affection for the Pueblo people. They were kind and gentle and were devoted to their children. They brought them to St. Catherine's School because they trusted that the sisters would teach them how to live good lives. It took some time to establish this trust and confidence. Mother Katharine, in her report to the community at the motherhouse, spoke of how the parents brought their children to the mission school. For the first day they would follow the child around. They looked over the classrooms, the dormitories, the dining area and all of the facilities. It was only after this inspection that they decided to leave their child in the custody of the sisters. When the mother decided to enroll her child at the school, Mother Katharine had the feeling that they were really doing the sisters a favor. After a few days they were telling their friends about how wonderful the sisters were and how well they treated their children.

The first mission opened by the Sisters of the Blessed Sacrament was a glorious success. For more than a century the successors of those pioneering sisters have continued to care for the spiritual and material welfare of thousands of New Mexico Indians. St. Catherine's School became an outstanding example of success for scores of other missions throughout the Southwest. Throughout her active career, Mother Katharine remained in constant contact with her first mission. The sisters and students always held a high place in her heart.

No one was happier than the foundress with the success of this first venture of a new congregation made up of young and inexperienced sisters. In one short year, they had taken a giant spiritual step. When she returned to Philadelphia, she met with Archbishop Ryan to review what had happened in Santa Fe. Those who knew the foundress, especially members of her own family, recognized how much she had grown. She had taken vows of poverty, chastity and obedience with a special concern for those races which had been so neglected during the years of church growth in this country. In that first year she proved what that vow meant to her community members.

The years of service that first mission school would give was summed up many years later by the Archbishop of Santa Fe. Shortly after the death of the foundress, Archbishop Edwin Byrne wrote these words to the new superior of the Sisters of the Blessed Sacrament: "I consider the presence of your daughters a distinct benediction for the Church in New Mexico, and it gives me joy to be able to express from time to time my gratitude to God and to them. May the Divine Missioner continue to bless St. Catherine's School for the Indians and may an intense love of souls animate always the spiritual daughters of Mother Drexel, who had fallen in love with immortal souls because she knew their value."

There was no question in the mind of Archbishop Ryan or in the minds of any of the Sisters of the Blessed Sacrament that Mother Katharine had begun a life of service to black and Native Americans. Her first year at St. Catharine's proved that to all.

When she returned to the motherhouse she heard some good news from Rome. The pope named her long-time friend, Father Joseph Stephan, a monsignor. He was a director at the Indian Bureau in Washington and from the beginning he encouraged the new foundress to come to the West to see first-hand the plight of Native Americans. The sisters celebrated his promotion and to please them he dressed in his new monsignor robes for a special Eucharist in St. Elizabeth's Chapel. Of course, a festive dinner followed.

All in all it had been an eventful year in the life of America's newest religious order.

Mother Katharine with her younger sister, Louise Morrell, and her dogs.

# CHAPTER 10

# VIRGINIA

In January of 1897, the Sisters of the Blessed Sacrament received good news from Rome. The Cornwells Heights community was delighted to hear that the Holy See had granted to the new congregation a "Decree of Praise." This was the first important step which would lead to the final approval of the Sisters of the Blessed Sacrament. The sisters had sought the help of Doctor Herman J. Heuser of St. Charles Seminary to formulate the constitution that would be approved in Rome.

Mother Katharine felt it would be a good idea to adopt the rule of the Sisters of Mercy and accommodate it to the more active missionary role her group had taken. When the rule and constitution were adopted at Cornwells Heights, they were sent to the Apostolic Delegate in Washington. In addition, letters from the bishops of every diocese in which the congregation had set up schools and convents were delivered to the delegate.

Archbishop Ryan assembled all of the necessary material. He also included a financial statement for the congregation and a list of all of the contributions of the Drexel Trust Fund. The report showed that Mother Katharine had generously contributed to 26 dioceses throughout the country. The new congregation prayed that as a result of all this information, they would receive final approval of the Holy See.

About this time, Cardinal Gibbons, as a spokesman for the Catholic bishops, petitioned the Congress to reopen the matter of contracts for Indian schools. Without the government's support, it was felt some of the schools would fail and there would not be sufficient funds to build new schools in the southwest where they were desperately needed. The commissioner had convinced the government leaders that they should cancel all support for religious schools unless they were placed directly under complete state control.

Those working in the Catholic Indian Bureau and superiors of other religious orders working among Native Americans came to the motherhouse to urge Mother Katharine to speak before the U.S. Senate. They urged her to give an account of the work of Catholic congregations and demonstrate how necessary their work with Native American youth really was.

The new foundress felt that she was not the one to make the public presentation in Washington. She urged Archbishop Ryan to step forth and make the case for the Catholic efforts to educate and prepare Native Americans for life in the 20th century. She promised the archbishop her support and that she and her sisters would, "Pray, pray, and pray some more." Finally the archbishop agreed to do as she asked.

In January of 1898, the archbishop of Philadelphia was formally invited to speak to the two houses of Congress and give his views about what our government policy should be. He had a forceful message. He outlined a brief history of schools for Native Americans. He approved of the plan of President Grant which through political maneuvering failed to live up to its promise for equitable distribution among the schools.

Archbishop Ryan made it clear that he came before Congress asking only one thing—that the government appropriation that would make it possible for the schools to survive be continued. They had proved clearly that they were efficiently operated and provided a good education.

He then spoke of the work of Mother Drexel. She had relied on the integrity of the government and its promises to help. Under the proposed regulations there would not only be a denial of allowances for children who attended mission schools, but they refused to permit parents to send their children to a Catholic school, even if this was their preference.

The archbishop warned the Congress that Mother Drexel could only help these children who were wards of the state, if the government would keep its word and help her. He concluded his message with these eloquent words, "These schools are needed for the government does not have nearly enough schools for all of the Indians, and I ask only that the United States fulfill the promises it made and keep the contracts."

Members of Congress and the press applauded his message openly but failed to grant his request. Little by little in the months and years ahead, the schools operated by the Sisters of the Blessed Sacrament and the other religious orders were deprived of almost all government support.

Mother Katharine and her sisters vowed that they would not give up the effort and would continue to provide their children with the best possible education without any help from the state. Truly it was a serious blow to all who were involved in the education of Native American youth.

One day in 1899, Monsignor Stephans appeared suddenly at the motherhouse in Cornwells Heights. He was much revered by the mother superior and for that matter by all who were concerned about the material and spiritual welfare of Native Americans. He told the sisters that he was about to celebrate on March 19, the 50th anniversary of his ordination as a priest. That is why he came unannounced to, in his words, escape from official Washington. The monsignor came to avoid a big anniversary celebration planned in his honor. He asked to stay at the motherhouse for a few days until it all blew over. This dedicated church leader, in his seventies and in poor health, was still actively engaged in fundraising to make up for the loss of funds as the result of congressional action. He presented Mother Katharine with a plan for providing funds for all the missionary congregations working with Native Americans.

While they were discussing how the pressing financial problems could be met, word arrived at Cornwells Heights that the cardinal archbishop of Baltimore, the apostolic delegate, and a half dozen other bishops were on the way to celebrate the anniversary at the motherhouse of the Sisters of the Blessed Sacrament. As Bishop Edmond Prendergast put it, "Since he would not stay in Washington, they all feel they must come to him."

It was a beautiful tribute to the aging missionary that the cardinal and a dozen bishops made the difficult trip to Pennsylvania to show him how much he meant to the Church in America. Cardinal Gibbons, Archbishop Martinelli, the apostolic delegate, Archbishop Ryan and the other prelates tried to put into words their gratitude to the embarrassed monsignor.

At their own private party, Mother Katharine and her sisters thanked their old friend for his many favors to the community. The superior, speaking on behalf of all, told Monsignor Stephans how grateful they were for his direction and told him that without his ever present guidance they would have accomplished little. To them, he was an unsung hero.

Meanwhile, the Sisters of the Blessed Sacrament had been invited by Bishop Augustine Vander De Vyver to come to the diocese of Richmond. The foundress' sister, Louise, and her husband, Colonel Edward Morrell, had purchased a large piece of property on the James River in the vicinity of Rock Castle, Virginia. It was located on a hill overlooking the river about seventy miles north of Richmond. From their own funds, they paid $28,000 for the almost 1,660 acre estate. On the property they built St. Emma's Industrial and Agricultural Institute. They chose this name to honor the memory of Louise's mother, Emma Bouvier Drexel. Louise and her husband were deeply interested in the education and spiritual welfare of black youth throughout the South. Virginia was the closest place in which a large number of black people lived. They came to the James

River area where poverty was a way of life for children of color. St. Emma's School would provide young blacks the opportunity to learn how to make a decent living. To accomplish this the Morrell family was willing to donate much time and a considerable amount of their extensive financial resources.

Louise was delighted to show her sister the huge tract of land they had purchased. Mother Katharine was impressed with the area. On a hill just opposite the Morell property, the Sisters of the Blessed Sacrament purchased about six hundred acres of land and prepared to begin the construction of St. Francis de Sales High School for girls. The beautiful new buildings were built on the crest of a hill overlooking the James River.

Once again, the superior chose to build a school in a remote spot which made it difficult to bring in supplies. The only way to reach the property was by train on the Chesapeake and Ohio Railroad which passed on the other side of the river. The way they could cross the river was by row boat or on a wooden flat that was owned by a neighbor. When those who designed the school recognized the transportation difficulties, they decided that much of the wood and the bricks could come from their own property. Once they decided to make use of native material, the construction was accomplished in a rather short period of time.

The two schools being built about the same time had many advantages. The schools were set on the top of twin hills with a half mile of beautiful meadow between them. It was especially helpful to have these two schools—one a high school for boys and the other for girls—so close together. Their close proximity made it possible to combine many of their efforts. In the years to come they would share special talents, social activities and faculty. Many of their most successful projects were accomplished with a team effort uniting both student bodies. In the fall of 1899, the new school was ready to begin operations. In July Mother Mercedes was

appointed superior and went with Mother Katharine to prepare the new building to receive its first students. The caretaker for the property met the sisters at the small train station. He ran over to the sisters to announce that, "Mothers, I
have very, very bad news for you. We have had an awful
fire."

At first the two mothers felt that the entire complex had
burned to the ground. When they reached the area, they discovered that it was the new barn that was destroyed. Much of
the burned out building was covered by insurance. The total
fire loss to the community was about $4,000—a considerable
amount in those days.

Far more serious than the monetary loss was the fact that the
police investigation indicated that the fire was intentionally set.
For the next several weeks that was in the back of the minds of
the two mothers. Who would want to do such a thing? In the
months ahead, would they try to do it again—on a much
greater scale? The authorities had no real answers to give.
Someone in that beautiful, pristine community was very angry
at the Sisters of the Blessed Sacrament for what they planned to
do at Rock Castle.

For the second time in their brief history, some disgruntled
neighbor had resorted to violence against a group of religious
women who were trying to live lives of holiness and service. As
with the stick of dynamite at the motherhouse groundbreaking,
so the fire at the opening of the new school cast a cloud over
what was to be a joyful celebration.

At the end of the summer, nine sisters left the motherhouse
to staff the new school in Virginia. When they arrived at the
sight, they could not believe such an imposing building could
be located in such a beautiful setting.

There was much work to be done. The young people coming to school in October had to be somehow classified by age
and education. For the first few years St. Francis de Sales was

to function as an industrial and normal school which would help students to become productive members of society. Girls of good quality were accepted. Within a short time it became a first class, fully accredited high school. Through the years thousands of young people from across the country came to Rock Castle for their high school education. Eventually the sisters charged a small fee.

It is interesting to note that just months before Mother Katharine died, a large renovation program and addition were completed at the cost of almost two million dollars. It was the last large building program conducted by the sisters because they ceased to have the Drexel Trust Fund to provide the necessary money to complete this kind of project.

Mother Katharine from the very beginning believed that her mission foundations were to be more that just schools for the children of the community. She was determined that they would be centers for Christians of all ages. In her Virginia foundation she accomplished this in several ways. From the start, she developed a program of home visitation. Despite the beauty of their surroundings, many of the people lived in abject poverty. During that first winter, the sisters spent some of their out-of-school time visiting these poor homes. They brought things that helped poverty stricken families somehow to get through the winter. They brought food, warm clothing, firewood and other useful gifts.

Not far from St. Francis de Sales School there was a State Prison Farm. The sisters made themselves known to the prisoners and began a program of religious instruction for the inmates. There were several successful conversions. In 1902 a condemned prisoner took instructions and was baptized a few days before his execution. One of the most appreciated features of this prison ministry was the small library that was set up on the farm. The inmates had the opportunity of having good reading material for the asking.

In an area in which there were few Catholics practicing their faith, the Sisters of the Blessed Sacrament determined that they would reach out to their neighbors in a social as well as religious way. These neighbors were invited to participate in concerts and lectures that lifted the mind as well as the spirit. In a few short years, St. Francis de Sales would become a cultural center for the James River community. The superior determined that she would form mission stations where the catechism could be taught, especially to the young blacks. On one of these trips to start a learning station, Mother Katharine looked out the train window and noticed what seemed to be a gleaming cross in the middle of the woods. None of the sisters had any idea what it was.

When they returned to the school, the superior was determined to find out what the cross meant. One of the students told her that there was a group of black people living in the village of Columbia in the area around a small wooden church. The two mothers decided to investigate the property. They found the church, cleaned up and polished. It could seat at least 200 adults. It was built by the Wakem family as a place where their priest-son could say Mass when on vacation.

The family was long since dead. The one black Catholic in Columbia began to take care of the building because he hoped that some day Mass would be celebrated there again. The sisters found the church and its black caretaker, "Uncle Zack Kimbro." Mother Katharine contacted Bishop Vander De Vyver and got his permission to conduct a Sunday school program there. Almost one hundred adults and children gathered weekly in the old church to learn about the Lord.

The numbers coming each week continued to increase. After about a year Uncle Zack had his wish come true. With special permission from the bishop, Mass was celebrated once a month in the old church in Columbia. Through a very strange set of unusual events, the Church of Jesus suddenly came alive again in that little corner of Virginia. In the first year, thirty adults and a number of young people were baptized in that little country church.

Each mission established by the Sisters of the Blessed Sacrament had its own unique contributions to make to the community. The school at Rock Castle became a model for others to follow. It was one of the first high schools in the country that was dedicated to providing Catholic girls with a superior secondary education. In the years to come, graduates of St. Francis de Sales High School had a profound effect upon the life of the Church in America. The sisters inspired hundreds of young women to enter the religious life and to play a leading role on the national scene, especially in the fields of education and health. It provided an ideal setting to inspire young girls with a sense of responsibility to the needs of others. Like the first mission in New Mexico, St. Francis de Sales School became an instant success. At the time of the first Christmas in Virginia, Mother Katharine wrote to her sisters and the girls in her new school these words: "You are there as Mary and Joseph to adore and worship and love Him in His first Christmas in St. Francis de Sales. Really I see little difference in one way, between his birth at Bethlehem and His birth in this land where He has never been before on Christmas day—the spot where my dear daughters will be at the Midnight Mass of 1899."

# CHAPTER 11

# ARIZONA AND BEYOND

B ack in 1896, after several requests from Monsignor Stephans, Mother Drexel agreed to finance the purchase of about two hundred acres of land in Arizona, about thirty miles from Gallup, New Mexico. The property was at the edge of a reservation for Navajos. They represented a very large and a very neglected portion of the American Indian population. Rather than send the Sisters of the Blessed Sacrament to staff this new missionary effort, Mother Katharine prevailed upon the Franciscan Fathers to set up a chapel and a mission. The Franciscan Provincial in Cincinnati sent Father Anselm Weber and a small group of religious to staff the new facility.

It was very difficult work. After years of poor treatment, the Navajos distrusted all white men and that in-cluded those in a religious habit. Father Weber and his companions tried hard to gain the trust of this large and sometimes warlike group of Native Americans. They made a great effort to learn their difficult language. They worked hard to gain additional supplies from the government and additional land from the Indian Bureau. The Navajos agreed to accept the white man's gifts but refused to accept the white man's God. The Franciscan Fathers would not give up. The entire mission, with all of its expenses, was paid for from the Drexel Trust Fund. Father Anselm reported to his bene-factor all of the problems the Franciscan missionaries were facing and what little progress was being made. After sever-al attempts to encourage the downhearted priest, Mother Katharine decided that she would go to the mission to see for herself firsthand.

Sister Agatha accompanied the superior in their first visit to the mission in Arizona. Father Anselm was away visiting the provincial house. Two young monks were gracious hosts and showed their visitors around the mission and the reservation. They explained their difficult relations with the Navajos and indicated that some progress had been made since they had for the most part learned how to understand the language. They also told the sisters that other religious denominations were having the same difficulties. Despite the many different groups working among them, they reported that they had never heard of a single Protestant Navajo.

In spite of their limited success, the Franciscans were still full of hope. The visitors from the East were all impressed by the Navajo tribe, especially with their wonderful native skills and the fascinating designs in their rugs, blankets and articles of clothing. Their iron and silver work showed them to be excellent craftsmen. Both the friars and the sisters saw a tremendous potential among the thousands of Navajos in Arizona and New Mexico.

The mission had great potential but Mother Katharine saw quite clearly that the building and facilities were far from adequate. She made some important decisions. The mission would be called St. Michael's. Monsignor Stephan suggested the name. He was convinced that the Navajo were a great nation and their sprawling tribe of thousands was ready to accept Christianity. For years he had been appealing to the Sisters of the Blessed Sacrament on their behalf.

Mother also directed that the building was to be expanded. She bought additional property for a school and convent. She went to the nearest town, Gallup, and engaged contractors to begin the work as soon as possible. She was full of enthusiasm for her newest mission.

She returned to the motherhouse and explained to Archbishop Ryan, the sisters and her contractor friends about the remarkable group of potential Christians she had met. They shared her excitement and looked forward to the speedy conclusion of her huge building project.

During the next few months the mother general was busy with many projects but managed to watch carefully the progress at St. Michael's Mission in Arizona. She soon realized that it was very difficult to supervise a large building project when you are almost two thousand miles away. She was convinced that things were going too slowly—far too slowly. By now, she was becoming a real traveler, frequently visiting old and new foundations. She was determined to visit the mission once again and to get things accomplished more quickly.

After five days in a railroad car, she and her companion, Mother Ignatius, were at the Gallup railroad station meeting the Franciscan superior Father Anselm. Once again Mother Drexel saw things firsthand and did not like what she saw happening.

The school was behind schedule. She complained to the contractor and things began to move again. Quickly things changed and it appeared that the job really could be finished in time for the fall school opening. She visited the reservations and had the opportunity to meet with parents whom she hoped would send their children to St. Michael's School. She found them concerned about their children and anxious to have them learn. With the superior among them, things seemed to take a more optimistic tone. She left the new mission this time far more confident than the last time. When she arrived back at the motherhouse, she explained to all who would listen how wonderful the Navajo people were and how wonderful their future would be.

She felt that the school would be off to a good start but was concerned about having her sisters in such a desolate spot. Outside of the school-convent complex, there was not much to be said about the territory. It was a land of rugged mountains and miles of treeless desert. Save for a few prosperous ranches, the Navajos lived in poverty. It was discouraging for the sisters to have to face this difficult terrain. They were determined to succeed and Mother Katharine was determined to provide the sisters and the Navajos a more pleasing neighborhood in which to live.

School did open on time. The children came in all sizes and all shapes and all ages. The teachers reported that as a group they were very shy and retiring. They were overwhelmed by the building—especially the size of the school. Their homes were so primitive that they could not believe the warmth and comfort of the classrooms and chapel. The sisters worked their magic and the children quickly responded to their acts of kindness and concern.

The first Christmas was a special time. The whole story was new to the Navajo youngsters and they found it to be appealing. The decorations and the little gifts were appreciated by those who had so little of this world's gifts. The moving celebration of the Christmas story had a profound effect that put a holiday glow on the bleak and rugged desert landscape.

As always, the sisters reached out also to the adults of the community. They were invited to come to the school and chapel during the Christmas season. They marveled at the altar decorated with boughs of pine trees. Surprisingly enough, it was the manger scene that caused somewhat of a problem for the Navajo women who had come to view the holiday scene.

It seems the sisters had been able to find only one figure for the crèche—that of the Bambino. One of the women was shocked. "Where is the baby's mother?" she cried out. She said she was worried because his mother had left him in a tiny crib with no quilt on to keep him warm.

Within a few years the problem for the Sisters of the Blessed Sacrament was reversed. In the beginning, they spent a great deal of time trying to persuade the parents to send their children to St. Michael's. It was not long before the school was overcrowded. There simply was no room to take care of all who applied and they pleaded with the sisters to enlarge their facilities in order to accommodate all their children.

In 1925 the tribal leaders got together and petitioned the superior to open a new school at another place. They asked this because they said, "All of us appreciate what you are doing for us and we would like all our children to attend a school like the school at St. Michael's, Arizona."

Mother Katharine found it impossible to fulfill their request. There were so many other demands upon the sisters and her limited funds. In the next few years, she did build a new gymnasium and buildings that added a good deal of classroom space. In 1946, a new high school department was added to St. Michael's. In 1948 the reconstruction of the entire plant was undertaken. A completely new high school campus was constructed. Both elementary and high school continued to operate with full classrooms.

It is said that when one crosses into Arizona on Route 87, one suddenly comes upon a huge campus of educational buildings, built in a sunken oasis. These buildings stand as a monument to the commitment of the foundress of the Sisters of the Blessed Sacrament to the Navajo nation. It is a commitment that has passed the test of time. For in the years since then, thousands of Native Americans have learned about God and His Church and have become productive members of the far-flung Navajo tribe, one of the largest nations in the land.

It was about this time that Mother Katharine became concerned by the huge sums of money that her congregation must spend just to keep up the missions and schools they had already begun. Monsignor Stephans suggested that she set up a large endowment fund for her congregation. She believed that the Lord would provide the security the sisters needed. She realized that once she died there would be no Drexel funds available. In a quandary as to what to do, she consulted a knowledgeable and holy Jesuit priest, Father Dominic Panatella. They decided not to try to develop an endowment fund but to trust that the Lord would provide in his own time. From that time on, she seemed no longer concerned about where the necessary funds would come from. She did in later years agree to set a small savings account for their mother-house, the education of sisters, and some support for the need-iest missions. After she died this proved to be a godsend for the community.

In the early months of 1904, Bishop Thomas Byrne of Tennessee wrote to Mother Katharine about the possibility of building a school for the poor blacks in the Nashville area. He had visited St.Catherine's School in Santa Fe and was much impressed. He told her he had picked out a site for a school and just wanted her to come down and look at it. She accepted the invitation and was delighted with the property and immedi-ately agreed to purchase it. She also promised that she would convert the present building into a school and a place for the sisters to stay. The new school would be called Immaculate Mother Academy. Bishop Byrne was delighted.

Unfortunately not too many of the Nashville citizens agreed with the bishop. For the first time in her career Mother faced organized opposition to her plans for providing decent schools for black children. Realizing that there would be objections for the planned use of the buildings, negotiations were held quiet-ly. The home was owned by a Nashville banker who did not realize that his family home would become a school for poor black children.

At a meeting with the realtors, Mother Katharine offered $24,000 for the property. Bishop Byrne added another $1,000 and the offer was accepted and the deed transferred. The bishop and the sisters rejoiced to know that they would be able to offer the black members of the community the opportunity for a good education.

A reporter for the Nashville Banner discovered the identity of the new owners and the use they planned to make of the facilities. When the people who lived in the area found out that a school for black girls was to be built in their part of town, they were for the most part horrified. It was one of the first occasions, but there be would be many more, when people would rise up and try to prevent the exercise of basic human rights because somehow that exercise would devalue their property.

The owner of the house wrote to the newspaper, Bishop Byrne and Mother Katharine, explaining that he did not know who purchased his property and had no idea what it was to be used for. He asked that the trade be rescinded and he offered to give back the entire purchase price. He could not tolerate the fact that his ancestral home was to become a school for black children.

Mother answered his letter and tried to reassure him that everyone would get along well. She wrote, "The Sisters of the Blessed Sacrament, who have purchased the property, are religious, of the same race as yourself. We will always endeavor in every way to be neighborly to any white neighbors in the vicinity; we have every reason to hope we may receive from our white neighbors the cordial courtesy for which Southern people are so justly noted."

The owner placed Mother Katharine's letter in a paid newspaper ad and then offered to allow the sisters to keep the property if they would turn it into a home for poor and aged blacks.

The tempest continued. An effort was made to build a new road that would run right through the house. Petitions were signed and letters were written to the local newspaper. A letter, signed by thirty women of Nashville, begged the sisters to use the building for anything but a school. The school, they added, "would cause terrible racial tension." They suggested that perhaps it would be better if the convent and school were built in a more rundown section of the city.

The whole situation was further complicated by a board of education proposal that black high schools should be eliminated. They would replace them by grouping all black high school students into some kind of a vocational institute which would help them find some meaningful kind of work as adults. As the sisters made final plans for renovating the building to prepare classrooms for the fall classes, things seemed to quiet down and many citizens were prepared to accept the fact that a Catholic high school for black girls would open in that building. Suddenly, violent opposition to the new school arose from a very unexpected source. One Sunday morning, from many of the black pulpits in the city, ministers preached urging parents not to send their children to the Catholic school. The Sisters stayed the course. School opened in the fall with 26 students. By the end of the first year, registration was over one hundred and the building was already too small.

The opposition ended completely when the case was thrown out of court. *The Nashville Banner* concluded its coverage of the turmoil with the words: "Bishop Byrne is to be congratulated for securing so fine a place for a school."

As years went by, Immaculate Mother Academy flourished. In 1907, a new school building was built and the student body grew. In a few more years the original building was condemned and another building project begun. Mother Katharine lived long enough to see the day in 1954 when the schools of Nashville were integrated. Immaculate Mother Academy closed and the Catholic boys and girls of the city, black and white, studied together in the new integrated Father Ryan

High School. Once again she had proven herself to be a pioneer for human rights—rights that go beyond the color of one's skin and the size of one's bankroll.

Mother Katharine and Sr. Xavier at Chinle, Arizona with Navajos.

# CHAPTER 12

# THE HOLY RULE

Early in 1907, Mother Katharine left the motherhouse for an eight-day retreat in solitude. The main purpose of these spiritual exercises was to discern the Lord's will as the Sisters of the Blessed Sacrament worked on the final version of their Holy Rule. This rule, if approved by the Holy See, would guide and direct members of the congregation in living the religious life. It is a document that took several years to construct and was approved by all the sisters. During these holy days, the foundress prayed for inspiration and prayed that the new Holy Father, Pope Pius X, would give his approbation to this important document.

The writing of a rule was a long and difficult process. As plans were being made for the new congregation, Bishop O'Connor was on hand for every important decision. The young foundress depended on his spiritual advice. After the new foundation began, she believed he would be available to direct them in formulating the new rule. His death delayed the process.

On guidance from Rome, the task began. The foundress selected the Rule of the Sisters of Mercy as a guide. Carefully she added several key factors which were unique to the new community. Several superiors, whose rule had already been accepted, offered their advice and counsel. When she completed the task, she sent the working copy to all the sisters at the motherhouse and the missions. She sought suggestions from those who would be obliged to live up to their rule.

After reading over the suggestions and putting them into a completed form, Mother Katharine Drexel sent the sisters the final draft and asked each sister to sign a copy indicating her approval of the proposal.

After the changes were approved by the sisters, Doctor Heuser made certain that each detail was in conformity with the Code of Canon Law. Archbishop Ryan gave his stamp of approval and the Holy Rule was sent to Rome for adoption. Instead, all the information was sent back to the motherhouse, indicating that a complete financial report had to be included. In addition to the expenses incurred by the congregation, the report was also to include the amounts that had been contributed to other dioceses and missions.

About this time the rector of the North American College, Monsignor Richard Kennedy, came to visit Mother Katharine. He was a native of the archdiocese of Philadelphia and proved very helpful. He talked about the delays in the Holy City especially with the new pope. He also said that Pope Pius X showed great interest in the Native American and black missions. The monsignor said he would bring pictures of the mission to show the Holy Father.

Finally, all seemed ready once again to send the Holy Rule to the authorities in Rome. One morning when the foundress was making final preparations, she was interrupted by an out-of-town visitor who introduced herself as Mother Cabrini of New York. She was the foundress of the Missionary Sisters of the Sacred Heart of Jesus.

They met for the first time but quickly became friends. Mother Cabrini had come to thank the Sisters of the Blessed Sacrament for their hospitality to her sisters. At dinner, Mother Katharine sought some advice. She inquired of the visitor whether or not she personally should take the Holy Rule to Rome. She realized that Mother Cabrini and the Sisters of the Sacred Heart had just recently gained approval of their rule. In answer to the inquiry Mother Cabrini gave this advice: "You see Mother, it is like this: We all get a lot of mail. Some things we must take care of immediately. Other items we put on the shelf for tomorrow. Tomorrow comes and we find ourselves busy doing something else. Before you know it, there are many items before it. That is the way it is in Rome. Things get shelved even though they are important. If you want to get your Holy Rule approved, take it there yourself and bring it back with you—approved."

Mother Katharine asked permission from Archbishop Ryan to go to Rome to obtain approval. He thought it was a great idea and happily gave his blessing to the project. And so, on May 11, 1907, she joined Mother James in a first-class cabin on the *Konigin Luise* and set forth for the Eternal City. They carried with them the copy of the Holy Rule.

Msgr. Kennedy met the travellers with some bad news. He was very busy and would not be able to meet with them for several days. He also told them that the priest he chose to translate the New Rule into Latin had died suddenly, and he did not know anyone who could converse with her in English and know enough about Latin to translate it into the official language. He asked them to come back in several days. The sisters were very upset and disappointed. They were facing what seemed to be another serious delay.

Suddenly, everything changed. Msgr. Kennedy met a priest from Philadelphia who had just completed work on a constitution for another congregation. He said he had the time and would be happy to help out some fellow Philadelphians in need. His name was Father Joseph Schwartz, CSSR, and he proved to be an excellent choice. Each day he met with the sisters at the North American College and they went over the constitution word by word. The sisters would copy the revised text each day and take it to a priest in the English College who would translate it into Latin. Actually, they found there was little to be corrected from the work of Father Heuser.

It took three weeks to accomplish this work and everyone was delighted with the final results. Since the two mothers had to wait for their interview with the Holy Father, they decided to spend some time visiting the shrines of Rome. They had a delightful time and it proved to be a spiritual adventure. At every church they visited, they prayed for the success of their mission. There were many holy hours made during these days in Rome.

The highlight of their stay in the Holy City was a private meeting with Pope Pius X. Msgr. Kennedy served as interpreter and they had a wide, long-range discussion. The pope was very interested in the work of the Sisters of the Blessed Sacrament and had a special concern for the needs of the poor, especially among the Native American and black populations. The Holy Father blessed the two mothers, the entire congregation, and all the people they served. Mother James brought with her a large tray of medals and religious articles to be blessed for the sisters of the congregation.

Cardinal Satolli informed the foundress that the Sacred Congregation would meet in the morning of July 6 to decide on their approval of the constitution. He told them they should spend that morning in prayer. They spent the time between 9:30 and noon assisting at Mass every half hour in St. Peter's. The following Tuesday the cardinal called to say that the constitution was approved and there were no substantial changes in the Holy Rule. The Holy Father quickly gave his official approval.

Happily Mother Katharine sent a cablegram to Archbishop Ryan and asked him to spread the good news to the whole community.

The delighted foundress and her companion booked passage for July 18 on the *Re d'Italia*. This ship was chosen because it had a chapel and Mass would be celebrated each day of the journey. The second reason why they chose this line was because they offered a substantial discount to religious. Coming over, because her sister Louise insisted upon it, they were booked on first class. This time they were on second class because they felt it more in keeping with the spirit of the Holy Rule toward the vow of poverty.

Among other things, the *Re d'Italia* was a slow ship. She told the sisters not to come to meet them in New York because this ship was never on time. She was right. It docked in New York four days late.

When they arrived in New York, they sent word to Cornwells Heights that they were on the way. When they reached the motherhouse, they were delighted to see almost the entire community gathered in the courtyard. Overhead there hung a huge sign in gold and white which read "Welcome to our Mother." Above all flew the papal flag. Mother Katharine was overwhelmed by the celebration. She led the group into the chapel where she said her prayers of thanks to God for all His gifts. She thanked Him for the safe journey home, for the approval of the Holy Rule and for the love of all her sisters.

As she knelt at the altar rail in prayer, the entire congregation joined in singing, "Holy God, We Praise Thy Name." Then she joined the sisters in singing her favorite hymn, *"Laudate Dominum Omnes Gentes."* She stood before the community to express her thanks. Tears poured down her face and she made no effort to conceal her deep emotion. For a moment she was at a loss for words. Finally she said, "Thanks, thanks, thanks, thanks."

According to the new constitution, as soon as it was approved the congregation should have a general chapter and live by the new Holy Rule for five years. After the passage of five years, the Holy Rule would be reviewed and the congregation would be formally approved by Rome.

The first general chapter of the Sisters of the Blessed Sacrament took place at Cornwells Heights on November 23, 1907. Of course, beloved Archbishop Ryan, now over 70, presided at the chapter ceremonies. The first chapter election was held and to the surprise of nobody, Mother Katharine was elected the first Superior General of the new congregation. In accordance with the new Holy Rule, Sister Mary Juliana was elected Mistress of Novices. This relieved the foundress from that position she had held since Mother Inez returned to the Sisters of Mercy.

This first general chapter marked the beginning of a new era of service for the Sisters of the Blessed Sacrament and a new Holy Rule. The first step in this new era would be reached after a five-year period to put the Holy Rule into practice. During this probational time, mother general, members of the congregation and church authorities would have the opportunity to evaluate how the rule worked and make any necessary changes.

Following the general chapter, Archbishop Ryan had some words of encouragement and advice for the celebrating sisters. He congratulated them on their great spirit of unity and urged them to foster that spirit in the years ahead. In his final remarks he said, "To you God commends his abandoned children. To you he says, 'Take these abandoned little ones as your own.' You shall spread yet more, have yet more vocations and the congregation, blessed by the benediction of the Holy See, shall have many, many chapters general."

As the celebration was ending, one of the sisters remarked that the new mother general was looking tired and pale. The sisters thought this might be so because she was not eating butter or sugar for Advent. The archbishop turned to the sisters and said, "As I read my office today, I am very impressed with the words of Isaiah."

Mother Katharine turned to listen to the spiritual wisdom that she was sure would fall from her spiritual director's lips. The archbishop went on, "Such a depth of meaning in the words of the prophet. Mother you know what Isaiah said, 'He shall eat butter and honey that he may know to refuse the evil, and to choose the good.' Do you eat plenty of butter, Mother?"

At this Mother Mercedes could not keep from chiming in,

"Your Grace, she has not eaten any butter in a long time, and we all think she needs it."

Mother Katharine answered, "Your Grace, my daughters are too anxious about me."

Turning to the new superior general, he said, "Well, maybe so, but you must promise me that you will do what the prophecy says."

At the evening meal, all eyes were on Mother Katharine as she said with a loud voice, "Sister, please pass the butter." With a smile, she took two helpings.

In the period immediately following the chapter, the Church gave its support to the missionary efforts aimed at the poor blacks throughout the South. Cardinal Gibbons in 1907 set up a Board of Colored Missions. Six bishops joined the board. Their goal was to raise funds and provide staff to work in black missions. Mother Katharine supported the board's work with a substantial donation. In the next few years, four schools for blacks were established in the greater Philadelphia area. Two of these were staffed by the Sisters of the Blessed Sacrament.

When Archbishop Ryan came to the motherhouse in February to celebrate the Superior General's feast day, the sisters were shocked to see how weak he seemed. He was unable to celebrate the Eucharist, but was happy to say a few words to the congregation. He blessed them and said, "Pray for the archdiocese and for me. For me because I am approaching eighty."

As he prepared for what he knew lie ahead, he called together all the major religious superiors under his jurisdiction. He expressed pleasure at the large number of congregations and praised the work they had accomplished in the archdiocese. His final words to the sisters were, "I want to ask you, dear Mothers, always to be kind to one another. Pray always to the Blessed Mother for the children under your care that they may be preserved from the evils of this age."

In the first week of February, the archbishop's secretary called the motherhouse asking the superior to come to visit the dying prelate. He was alert enough to recall to mind details of their long friendship and how much had been accomplished. She reminded him of the time, following the death of her mentor Bishop O'Connor, when she came to him she was almost ready to leave the convent. She recalled he asked her, "Could you go on if I promised to help? Tell me if I promise to be your father in God and tell you to come to me when you need help, then do you think you would be able to stay?"

For more than twenty years, the archbishop kept his promise and was always ready to guide and help. When he died, Mother Katharine was devastated. Brokenhearted, she realized more than ever what his presence meant to the Sisters of the Blessed Sacrament.

John Patrick Ryan, the second archbishop of Philadelphia, accomplished much for his archdiocese. He is rightly remembered for establishing 82 new parishes, and building scores of schools and hospitals. He was a noted orator, theologian, and educator. But he will be remembered most of all for the love, guidance and direction he gave to the saintly foundress of the Sisters of the Blessed Sacrament. On his deathbed, he told his spiritual daughter that he considered himself to be a co-founder of the congregation.

The archbishop died on February 11, 1911. Thousands filled the streets of Philadelphia to mourn his passing. At St. Elizabeth's in Cornwells Heights, his religious family gathered to celebrate the Eucharist thanking God for sharing Archbishop Ryan with them. Archbishop John Glennon of St. Louis gave the eulogy. His words concerning Archbishop Ryan could have been spoken also about his spiritual daughter, Mother Katharine. "In the symphony of sorrow, the children of the white race can hear the low refrain of the black man's grief and the stoic calmness of the red man's sorrow, for those were the races whose cause he championed and whose souls he would save."

Throughout the archdiocese of Philadelphia, many hearts were filled with grief but at St. Elizabeth's Motherhouse the grief was deepest of all. For among the Sisters of the Blessed Sacrament, it was truly the grief of a family that had lost a loving father.

Mother Katharine stayed in mourning until after the funeral at Our Lady of the Blessed Sacrament Convent which she had founded a few years earlier. Throughout the day of the funeral, her tears flowed freely. During supper, in a tearful voice, she asked the sisters' pardon, and she added that she would not want them to think that her tears somehow meant that she had lost her vocation of service, but added that she simply could not stop the tears.

Quickly the Holy See appointed Bishop Edmund Prendergast as the third archbishop of Philadelphia. He had been the auxiliary bishop for some years and was well known to the sisters at Cornwells Heights. He had also served as pastor of St. Malachy's Church which had the largest black population in the city. He had been much involved in the cause of social justice and was very sympathetic and supportive of the work of Mother Katharine and her sisters.

One of his first visitation stops as the new archbishop was at St. Elizabeth's Convent. After a personal talk with the superior general, he gathered together all the sisters at the motherhouse. He spoke to them about their association with his predecessor. He took the opportunity to tell them of his strong support of their work. He indicated to them that, like Archbishop Ryan, he would be there when they needed him. His reassurances were greatly appreciated by the sisters and especially Mother Katharine. During his days as archbishop, he proved to be faithful to his word.

# CHAPTER 13

# MISSION TO THE NORTH

Shortly after the death of Archbishop Ryan, the congregation began preparation for the final approval of the Holy Rule. There was to be a five-year trial to test the effect the rule had on the growth of the congregation. If approval was granted by the Holy See, the probation period would be over. The new rule would be permanent.

In view of her success in obtaining the temporary constitution, Monsignor Kennedy thought that it would be best that the mother general herself bring the rule to Rome. Archbishop Prendergast gave his immediate approval of the trip. In the meantime, the monsignor was consecrated a bishop and sent to spend some time in the United States. Realizing he would not be in the Holy City when the approbation would take place, he assigned Father Schwarz to handle the case. The bishop told the sisters that "Father Schwarz in matters of this kind is much more efficient than I am."

Father Schwarz reported to the mother general from Rome that all was in readiness for her arrival in the coming November. He was confident for a successful mission. Back at Cornwells Heights, she began to make preparation for the Roman trip.

Before her trip to Rome, Mother Katharine decided that she would like to make a visitation at St. Catherine's School in Santa Fe and stop off at her new school in Chicago. Some councilors objected to this plan. They urged that she give up any missionary trips for the rest of the year so that she could concentrate on her trip to Rome and the final approval of the Holy Rule. She insisted that she felt fine and decided to add a stop in Cincinnati where she had been asked to open a mission. With her usual confidence and enthusiasm, she started out on her missionary journey.

But somehow the Lord had other plans.

It began on September 24 when Mother James received a telegram from Santa Fe asking the community to pray very hard for a special intention. The intention was not named. A few days later the whole congregation was upset with the news that Mother Katharine had a cold, and on examination the doctor found some congestion in a lung. In an effort to make light of the problem, she told the sisters that her doctor wanted her to come down from the high altitude and placed her in the Albuquerque Sanitarium.

She also admitted that she had the beginnings of typhoid. She quickly added that she had the services of a trained nurse and a good doctor. She absolutely forbade anyone coming to see her. She told the sisters that it would be a five-day journey and by that time she would be feeling better. The nurse reported that she took the whole situation quite calmly. After hearing the news about the typhoid fever, she got into bed and said, "Well, I feel perfect peace on an occasion like this, as it is certainly not according to my plans, and it must be God's Will."

It certainly seemed to be God's will that Mother Katharine would not be going to Europe anytime in 1912.

Back at the motherhouse, Mother James was also ill. She asked Archbishop Prendergast if, despite the order, he would allow her to send two sisters to Santa Fe. The archbishop did not think that was a good idea because it would do more harm than good. He was very concerned and told the sisters if it became necessary, he would go himself.

Quickly the news of Mother Katharine's illness spread throughout the nation. Bishops, missionaries, and those being served by the congregation wrote to the sisters promising prayers for a speedy recovery.

Suddenly, her brother-in-law, Colonel Morrell, took over. Immediately he left for Santa Fe. In a few days he reported to the motherhouse that "I have seen Kate. She is much gratified at my arrival. Typhoid symptoms rapidly decreasing and lungs are clearing up. Temperature is normal, pulse good, she sends her love."

The Colonel made sure that certain tests were taken. Quickly he made plans that the patient be moved out of the bad climate. He arranged for a special private car of the Atchison, Topeka and Santa Fe Railroad. Mother Loyola, some nurses and Colonel Morrell traveled with her. He had included on the train an oxygen tank and the latest medical equipment in case of emergency. None was needed and they reached the mother-house without incident.

The Colonel called in two prominent specialists to give her a complete examination. They concluded that indeed she did have typhoid and bronchial pneumonia and was on the verge of a nervous breakdown. They made it quite clear to all that only complete rest would bring about a complete recovery.

At first she made a joke of her confinement and all the rules and regulations. In a few days, recognizing the gravity of the illness, Mother Katharine became a most cooperative patient. The doctors gave strict instructions and insisted that they be observed to the letter. She was not to transact any business, to see anyone except her doctors and nurses, or to walk anywhere. She was even forbidden to go to the chapel.

The collapse and the huge interruption of her plans upset her greatly. Quickly, she recognized God's will—as she always did—and her recovery began. All of the sisters recognized that it would take time. As a matter of fact, it was December before she was allowed to have sisters visit, and almost Christmas before she was allowed to assist at Mass.

By the end of the year, she became more like her old self with all of the traces of her illness gone. With the approval of her doctors, she rescheduled her trip to Rome to early April.

In the meantime, requests for help from the Sisters of the Blessed Sacrament continued to grow. The North and the Midwest became centers of attention. Much was accomplished at the January meeting of council. They went over again the Holy Rule in its final form before it would be submitted to Rome. They voted to purchase two large building lots in New York City and made plans to construct a school for five hundred students. They accepted an invitation from Cardinal William O'Connell to set up a catechetical center in the Worcester Square section of Boston.

Having settled all outstanding business with a flurry of activity, she decided to set sail for Rome in early April. The foundress was accompanied by Mother Mercedes and a pilgrimage from the diocese of Toledo. She chose the ship because Bishop Joseph Schrembs and eighteen priests were on board and she knew there would be many opportunities to assist at the celebration of the Eucharist.

The two sisters enjoyed the ocean voyage. They found a peaceful place on the deck removed from the other passengers. Here they could read some books, say some prayers, and discuss their coming interviews with members of the Roman canonical authorities. They and all of the congregation were pleased with their experience with the Holy Rule. They were confident that it would get final and permanent approval.

Not only did the sisters have the opportunity for daily Mass during the voyage, they also had the opportunity to take part with the bishop in the celebration of the Feast of Corpus Christi. This festive Mass was followed by the Eucharistic procession from the chapel through the center of the ship to the bishop's cabin. Here adoration of the Blessed Sacrament and Benediction were celebrated. Delighted with the celebration, Mother Katharine told the bishop that her two hours of adoration were the highlight of the ocean voyage.

Following their arrival at Naples, they took a train to the Holy City. They were met by Lucy Drexel Dahlgren, a wealthy cousin of the foundress. Mrs. Dahlgren offered to have the nuns stay at her home. She had leased Barberini Palace. She offered her cousin her own apartment across the street from the Church of the Capuchins. She also offered the services of a maid and chauffeur. Mother would have liked to stay next to the church, but thought that the quarters were too luxurious for two nuns who had taken the vow of poverty. The sisters stayed in modest rooms in the Cenacle.

The visitors to Rome were disappointed to find out that Pope Pius X was ill and unable to conduct any audiences. In his stead, Raffelo Cardinal Merry del Val conducted a long interview with the sisters. He told them that the pope had signed all the necessary papers of approval and blessed a long list of people they had recommended in his prayers. The cardinal, on his own behalf, asked the mother general this question: "Do you feel that work among the Negroes of the United States is in any way useless and unproductive?"

The Annals of the Congregation of the Blessed Sacraments report that a startled Mother Katharine protested, "Oh, no, Your Eminence, not once have we felt that. It is wonderful to work with them and very rewarding."

The relieved cardinal said, "I have heard Americans say that this work is useless, but I found it hard to believe."

The final approval of the constitution and rule were given in March. Interestingly enough, the decree called for only one change—a change of the official name of the congregation that was suggested by the foundress herself. The original name was the Sisters of the Blessed Sacrament Pro Indis et Negrites (for Indians and Negroes). The new name was changed to Pro Indis at Populis Coloratis (for Indians and People of Color). Once again, Mother Katharine demonstrated that she was a woman far ahead of her time.

Their important business finished, the sisters decided that they would visit some schools, convents and mission centers on the continent. They spent a brief time in Germany and Switzerland learning about educational methods used by the local religious orders. As a result of their conversations, in the next few years two young German women came to America and joined the Sisters of the Blessed Sacrament. They concluded their tour in Ireland where Father John Murphy, CSSP, acted as their guide. An old friend of the congregation, he introduced the Americans to the Irish view of religious education for elementary school students. The brief trip to Ireland resulted in two more vocations for the congregation. It also started the custom of sending two sisters to visit Irish schools on an annual basis. The result was scores of vocations to work in the Native American and black missions.

Before their return to America, Lucy Dahlgren accompanied the sisters as they visited the churches, shrines and holy places of the city. As the trip to Rome ended, the visitors were exhausted but delighted over what had been accomplished. They returned to Cornwells Heights with the Church's approval of their work. A joyful *Te Deum* was sung in the chapel on June 20 as the congregation rejoiced.

Shortly after her return from her successful mission in Rome, Mother Katharine was forced to deal with a frightening demonstration of racism and bigotry in her own country.

In 1912 Father Ignatius Lissner, S.M.A., opened a large mission in the city of Atlanta, Georgia. Funds for the large building project were given to Father Lissner by Mother Katharine Drexel. She asked that the mission be placed under the Patronage of Our Lady of Lourdes in honor of Archbishop Ryan who died on her feast day. Mother had intended to send some sisters to Atlanta to staff the mission. When the word about this got around, an enormous amount of opposition developed and threats were made against the school. When this happened, Father Lissner and the mother general decided to staff the school entirely with lay teachers.

After waiting for a year, the priest reported that opposition to the Catholic school had died down. On his suggestion, Mother Katharine sent a few of her sisters to join the faculty. The neighbors made every effort to make life miserable for the sisters. An amazing fact rose to the surface. It became clear to all that the people of the city were not so concerned about religious sisters teaching in the new school as they were with black children being taught at all.

Once it became known that the Sisters of the Blessed Sacrament were planning to open a second mission in Georgia, opposition to the sisters spread throughout the state. Macon, the site of the new mission, became a hotbed of opposition. This opposition became so intense that a group of legislators tried to make their form of bigotry a matter of law. Their proposal would make it illegal for any white teacher to teach in any school for colored children in the state of Georgia. It would also prohibit any colored teacher from teaching in a school for white children. To violate the provisions of this bill would be a crime. Fortunately, the bill never saw the light of day.

Archbishop Prendergast stepped forward to charge that the proposed bill was patently unconstitutional, and suggested that a forceful protest should be made by people of every race and religion. In a statement to Catholics and other people of good will throughout the state of Georgia, he presented the issue in unambiguous terms. In a public statement he said, "If there are any others who are concerned about this issue, we should make common cause with them. If not, then we must make the fight alone. To be silent in fear of exciting bigotry, it seems to me, is acting cowardly. Every intelligent Catholic in Georgia must realize that this issue is of vital importance and we must protest forcibly against the passage of this bill."

When the first reading of the bill was held in the state legislature, the state's largest and most influential newspaper, the *Atlanta Constitution* came out in protest. In a petition sent to the legislature, a group of Georgia citizens wrote, "This bill would be class legislation of the worst kind. It is unchristian and anti-missionary. The law of Georgia would say: Teach white people only. God's law says: teach all people."

The broad-based opposition of the people of Georgia carried the day. After the second reading of the bill, it was immediately rejected by the legislature.

Outright acts of bigotry never seemed to phase or deter Mother Katharine in her fight for social justice. She was heartened by the support of religious and civic leaders and by the leading newspapers. Over and over again, the vast majority of the American people supported her efforts on behalf of human rights.

She also took consolation in the fact that most of her efforts to build schools for the disadvantaged children of an area were welcomed with enthusiastic support by the community. When her new school opened in St. Louis, there was no opposition of any kind, and the school was immediately filled with students. In Cincinnati, all realized the demand was so great that they would have to add on to the newly built mission. Such was the reaction throughout the middle west and northern states.

In the midst of these great success stories, the mother general turned her attention to the largest center of disadvantaged children. She turned to teeming Harlem with its thousands of underprivileged black children who were being deprived of equal educational opportunities. To learn more about the problems and the enormous opportunities, she and her efficient assistant, Mother Ignatius, made what they called "a missionary journey" to New York City. What they found was a mind-boggling missionary opportunity. While a Catholic school system was flourishing in the greater New York area, the predominantly black Harlem community was being neglected.

The first missionary journey was not a success. In the heat of summer, the two mothers walked the streets from storefront to storefront and could not find a building that could be used as a convent or school. They had to give up the search in order to take part in the community retreat in the motherhouse.

As soon as the spiritual exercises were completed, the two mothers returned to continue the search. This time they stayed at the Religious of the Sacred Heart in suburban Manhattanville. They decided to concentrate on the district between West 125th Street and West 142nd Street. They were on the lookout for two suitable buildings—one to house the sisters and the other to serve as a school.

Each day they would hit the pavement at 8 a.m. and walk the streets until 6 p.m. In the hot New York sun, they would climb the stairs from the basement to the third or fourth floor and down again. In reality, these two mothers became the first of scores of Sisters of the Blessed Sacrament who have walked the streets of Harlem on behalf of the poor black children of the community. Eventually there would be five schools taught by the daughters of Mother Katharine in the Harlem area. Even until this day, the sisters walk the streets and give witness to their concern for the education of all of God's children.

After weeks of effort, their search ended one hot summer afternoon on a block on West 134th Street. Opposite each other on the same street, the sisters discovered two houses that could fill their needs. The larger house, in good condition, was what they wanted for a school building. Across the street a smaller building which was in need of repair and cleanup, could be used as a convent. Realizing that these buildings were not ideal, the mother general decided to rent them and continue to look for a more permanent site to purchase.

When arrangements were made, the call went out to the motherhouse and several sisters were sent to help with the enormous cleanup operation. Clean up they did. The new school and convent were open that fall and the Sisters of the Blessed Sacrament began what would be a long and fruitful ministry in New York, the city with the largest minority population in America.

# CHAPTER 14

# THE MIRACLE OF NEW ORLEANS

The website of Xavier University proudly proclaims: "There are 102 historically black colleges and 253 Catholic colleges in the United States, yet only one is both black and Catholic. That distinction belongs to Xavier University of Louisiana, which strives to combine the best attributes of both its faith and its culture." Those who are familiar with the Church and its relationship to the black community in Louisiana, often refer to Xavier University with its almost four thousand students—more of whom are Baptist than Catholic—as "The Miracle of New Orleans."

The first out-of-town visitor to Mother Katharine in her temporary novitiate in Torresdale in 1891 was Archbishop Francis Janssens of New Orleans. He had come seeking help for his debt-ridden archdiocese. His sincerity greatly impressed the new superior. After his return to his archdiocese, there began a long series of letters from the archbishop describing the great poverty of the black population of Louisiana. Mother, through the Drexel Trust Fund, responded with generous gifts that made it possible for the archbishop to build schools and missions, and to help meet the needs of his neglected poor.

Through the mail, they became good friends. The mother general visited the churches and schools she helped to support and marveled at the work the dedicated archbishop had accomplished on behalf of the poor blacks in his archdiocese. She praised Archbishop Janssens and kept his missionary efforts in her prayers. The needs of the Church in Louisiana were close to her heart, but it would be long after the archbishop's death before the Sisters of the Blessed Sacrament would be active members of the New Orleans community.

It was in 1913 that Archbishop James H. Blenk, the archbishop of New Orleans, first wrote to Mother Katharine to seek help in the education of the huge black population of Louisiana. The dedicated archbishop was anxious to provide an education for the thousands of blacks who got little or no schooling at all. He told mother that it would be a great opportunity for her congregation to make a real contribution, and urged that she consider setting up a mission in his archdiocese. She agreed with the archbishop and packed her bag for New Orleans.

The mother general already had a good idea about conditions in the delta country because for years she had been sending financial assistance to help support a black school that she had built several years earlier. With her assistant, Mother Mercedes, she decided to see firsthand what the situation was like in Louisiana. She found the archbishop was a sickly old man with a sharp mind who was looking for ways to improve the lot of his poor and uneducated people. He told his visitors from the north that since the close of the Civil War, he estimated that close to forty thousand blacks in his diocese no longer practiced their faith. Those ex-slaves who could afford it sent their young people North to receive an education. Most of them were forced to remain in the South where schools for blacks were in deplorable condition. The archbishop was overcome with the enormous problem he faced.

Archbishop Blenk pleaded with the mother general to help. He told her that he had so much to do and had such little strength and resources with which to work. He said that his life was coming to an end and the black people of Louisiana had turned to him for help. In desperation, he turned to the Sisters of the Blessed Sacrament as his only hope for success.

The old and sickly archbishop had a remarkable, almost revolutionary plan. He told mother that she was the only one in the world that could bring it into reality. He had thought about

it long and hard but never had the resources to even get it started. Educational leaders, in and outside the Catholic community, shook their heads and considered the project a pipe dream
of a man who was not living in the real world.

At this point one of his assistants told the archbishop that it
would require a miracle to make his ambitious plans come
true. Later on, when in reality they did come true, many people called it a miracle.

Mother Katharine listened to the old man's dream.

The archbishop explained to mother that there was little
progress in an effort to educate the poor black children for eco-
nomic, social and legal reasons. The laws and traditions of the
state of Louisiana provided no teachers to educate the poor
black students. Many in the community believed that they
should not be educated. Others, including many Catholic leaders, felt that the responsibility for providing schools for black
students rested with the black population. Neither the necessary financial support nor the qualified black teachers were
available. The result, in the words of Archbishop Blenk was
that "Our poor colored get only the leftovers—if there are any."

Since the need was great to have qualified black teachers to
teach black children as soon as possible, the archbishop wanted to open in the city of New Orleans a high school for black
boys and girls. The school would have the best of study courses and also the best of teachers.

The two mothers listened with amazement as the old archbishop continued to outline his plan. With the success of the
high school program, it was his hope that the graduates would
form a trained student body for a teachers' college on the same
site. Graduates of the college could then teach the poor black
children on the elementary school level. As if that were not
enough, he concluded the description of his dream for the
future. With a hushed voice he said, "Perhaps someday, we
may have a great university for our colored Catholics."

To his astonishment, Mother Katharine did not seem the least bit reluctant to give her approval to this most ambitious project that would radically change the direction of Catholic education in Louisiana for years to come. There were still many critics who were convinced that it was all a hopeless and impossible dream. But with the combination of the vision of the venerable archbishop and the past track record of the mother general, many began to see the possibility that some day it would all come true.

God worked in strange ways to bring it all about. At the time the archbishop and the mother general were dreaming, things were happening in the State Legislature which would help to bring about the fulfillment of their dream.

Southern University, a state owned college, was situated on the banks of the Mississippi River in the outskirts of New Orleans. Some black children enrolled in the university and many black families moved into the area. The middle and upper class whites resented the black invasion of the area. They petitioned the State Legislature to move Southern University to Scotlandville. Black Catholic leaders fought the move, but to no avail. The transfer quickly took place and a new university was built.

The huge and impressive building that was once the home of the prestigious Southern University was now empty. In 1915, the vacant college building was put up for sale. The main building and a smaller, two-story house were in excellent condition. There was a large auditorium, ten classrooms, a laboratory and offices. It would take very little time to prepare the buildings for the four hundred students that the archbishop expected in the fall.

Archbishop Blenk negotiated with the state officials and they agreed to sell Southern University for $18,000. The first part of the dream quickly became a reality.

For years the Drexel Family Trust supported small black schools in the New Orleans area. The superior general decided against sending her sisters to teach in these schools. This new venture, the largest to be undertaken by the sisters, represented a special challenge. Sisters were sent from the motherhouse, and the enrollment of students began in what was to be called Xavier Academy.

Things were happening quickly. Mother Katharine concluded negotiations for the purchase of the building. Repairs and relatively minor alterations were begun immediately. She poured over catalogues and courses of study from the old university. She decided to continue in that tradition of preparing young men and women as future teachers. The core of her educational program was to impart knowledge of God and the responsibilities and duties of Christian living. Each day she became more and more enthusiastic about the huge project she had undertaken. She looked forward to the day when young black graduates, with teaching degrees, would staff the small schools already in place and the many more that would be built in the years to come.

She arranged with Archbishop Blenk that a new parish be established at the site. The building contained a 500-seat auditorium that would make an excellent chapel for the students and a chapel for the black Catholics in the neighborhood. Father John Clarke was appointed the first pastor. In a very short time it became a flourishing parish, and it was not long before he supervised the construction of a separate church building for what was to be called Blessed Sacrament parish.

A friend of the archbishop, John McInerney, actually purchased the property. When the identity of the real owners of the buildings became known in the community, many of the neighbors were furious. All their efforts—including their appeal to the State Legislature to move Southern University—backfired. Instead of removing the black students from the neighborhood, more and more of them poured into the area to enroll in the new school, and to become part of a new Catholic parish for blacks.

Their anger and resentment were too late. The miracle was underway. The archbishop and mother general were convinced that the word "Southern" cut into the stone across the top of the building would soon be replaced with the words "Xavier University."

The people of New Orleans found it hard to believe that in a few months the building that housed the largest state university in Louisiana would become a Catholic high school for black students. In August, Mother Mercedes and Sister Francis were sent to help get things ready for the fall opening. Sister Francis was named director of studies. She decided that for the first year there would be four grades: seventh, eighth, ninth and tenth. Another decision was made that the faculty should be integrated from the very beginning. Five black teachers were immediately hired.

On September 21, registration day was a fantastic success. Before the day was over it became quite clear that additional classes would have to be set up. Among the applicants were 34 eleventh grade students who refused to enroll in any other local high school. The quick decision was made to add an eleventh grade to the new school.

Archbishop Blenk had predicted that in a few years Xavier Academy would have four hundred students. At the end of the first registration, the new school had already enrolled 320 full time students, more than one hundred afternoon and evening students, and several classes on a normal school level for school graduates. The total enrollment for the first year of operation was almost five hundred students. Even the archbishop was amazed with the enrollment figures.

The first faculty consisted of five sisters and six lay teachers. As had been a custom from the beginning of the Sisters of the

Blessed Sacrament, Sister Francis reported back to the mother-house on a regular basis. From the start it was noted that there were no disciplinary problems. The students were anxious to have the opportunity to learn and quickly applied themselves. The numbers kept increasing and the sisters were very reluctant to turn away young people who were so anxious to learn.

The growth of the school astonished the New Orleans community. In 1916, the twelfth grade was established. But, as the archbishop had predicted, there was no stopping. In 1917, a two-year normal school program was put in place. This became a necessity not only because so many students wanted to continue their studies, but also because the state of Louisiana passed legislation requiring that black teachers must have completed two years of normal school training. Up until then, all the black teacher had to do was to pass a test to gain a certificate to teach.

The new school was quickly appreciated by the black families in the area. Parents were most cooperative with the faculty and helped in any way they could. Many were attracted to the new Blessed Sacrament Parish, and several families were under instruction and would soon be converts to the Catholic faith.

Mother Katharine returned to the motherhouse delighted with the early results of the mission to New Orleans. Before she left, she had the opportunity to talk with Archbishop Blenk about the second step in his plan to educate the black children of his archdiocese. They began to formulate the start of a new two-year normal course, so that those who graduated from the academy would have the opportunity to continue their studies in a Catholic atmosphere. Upon the conclusion of the program, they would be able to be certified by the authorities to teach in the state of Louisiana.

When she got back to Cornwells Heights, the mother general was delighted to hear that her cousin Lucy Drexel Dahlgren wanted to join the Sisters of the Blessed Sacrament as a postulant. She was certain that God had called her to follow in the Drexel tradition of a life of service to God's poor and disadvantaged children.

In 1918, the second phase of the dream became a reality. A two-year normal school program was officially added to Xavier Academy. Since the beginning, informal classes were held in the evenings. The formal program, which conformed to the official curriculum established by the state of Louisiana, was open to all high school graduates. Registration day filled the classroom space that was available. To provide space, meeting rooms were improvised. It was apparent from the first day of classes that the normal school program filled an enormous need. Once again, the families of the young people rallied to support the sisters in every way possible. Scores of graduates from the two-year program began to fill the teaching positions available in the small schools of the delta country. These new young teachers made it possible for many hundreds of poor black children to receive the education they needed so desperately.

Many graduates of the normal school began to express a desire for a traditional college degree. Mother and her associates began to revise the normal school program to begin to provide some regular college courses that would lead to a bachelor's degree. In the fall of 1925, the third phase of the dream became a reality when Xavier was formally established as a College of Liberal Arts and Sciences. In 1928 the college conferred its first degrees.

The remarkable history of Xavier from the day it enrolled its first seventh grader in the Academy in 1915, until the day the college conferred its first bachelor's degree in 1928, took only thirteen years. Although this remarkable feat would not qualify as a miracle according to church requirements, the people of Louisiana and educational leaders throughout the country have referred to Xavier University as "The Miracle of New Orleans."

Within a very few years it became quite clear that the college would have to separate from the high school building and have enough room to expand. It was not easy to find a new college site in the city. Finally the mother general had to go into an area without zoning, and she purchased a five-block long piece of land on a canal with a railroad track in back of it.

As soon as the property was purchased, the serious task of changing this drab, wet and unattractive piece of land into a modern university began in earnest. When the task was finished, in the center of the property stood a large Indiana limestone administration building that has become a city landmark. There was a well-equipped science building, a convent for the Sisters of the Blessed Sacrament, and a football stadium completed the original foundation. The stadium was required because the black students were not allowed to play or practice on town-owned fields. Quickly, a college library, men's dormitory, women's dormitory, student center and chapel soon followed. In September of 1932, the student body moved into the mid-town college campus. The complex was dedicated the next month with Cardinal Dennis Dougherty presiding at the ceremonies attended by thousands of New Orleans citizens— black and white—who had come to celebrate the fulfillment of a dream.

Fittingly, the street address of Xavier University of Louisiana is 1 Drexel Drive in New Orleans. The campus is located in what is today the center of the city, less than a mile from the Louisiana Superdome. Today, the university is made up of 3,655 full-time students, 41 buildings and more than 12,000 alumni. Its impact on the black population of this country is enormous. For example, of the 6,500 black pharmacists in the United States, 25% of them graduated from Xavier School of

Pharmacy. The university ranks first in the nation in placing blacks in medical schools.

The impact of the university has been described in many national magazines and newspapers. *The New York Times Selective Guide to Colleges* has observed that "Xavier is a school where achievement has been the rule, and beating the odds against success a routine occurrence."

At the time of the canonization of Mother Drexel, Norman C. Francis, the president of Xavier University, was questioned as to why his school was often referred to as "The Miracle of New Orleans."

He is quoted in the *Philadelphia Daily News* as saying, "We certainly appreciate the Church's recognition of the physical miracles attributed to St. Katharine's intercession. But people here have recognized her as a saint for a long, long time. She changed lives for the better on a daily basis. At Xavier, she gave hope where there was little or no hope. Isn't that a miracle?"

# CHAPTER 15

# MISSION TO THE BAYOUS

The outstanding success at Xavier encouraged others in the New Orleans area to come to the Sisters of the Blessed Sacrament for their help in providing for the huge number of young black boys and girls. In the days following the establishment of the college, the educational needs of the state of Louisiana claimed a large part of the time, resources, and talent of the sisters.

In a few short years the sisters established a total of six parish schools within the city. All of them flourished and were filled to capacity with black students who were most willing learners. Outside of New Orleans, mother general established schools in the towns of Lake Charles, Rayne, Eunice, Carencro, Church Point and St. Martinville. Soon, hundreds of disadvantaged children were receiving a Christian education in a series of small schools scattered in the villages and bayous in delta country.

It was clear that more rural schools were needed. The most desperate educational needs were in those bayou communities where there was deep poverty among the whites and abject misery for the poor blacks. Monsignor Emil Jeanmard, the chancellor of the archdiocese, explained to the mother general that schools had to be placed in these small bayou villages. If the schools were not right in these bayous, it would be impossible for the children to attend because there was no transportation between villages. Now that she saw the gravity of the problem, she was ready to help in any way possible.

There was one remarkable priest who was working full time among the poor in the delta country. His name was Father Jean Marie Girault de la Corgnais. He was a romantic French folk hero who was idolized by those who lived in the bayous. It is said that he was a member of a noble French family. He gave up being a count to live in utter poverty among the poor trappers and hunters who lived along the banks of the Mississippi River.

Father Girault had served in the Cathedral Parish of New Orleans. A visit to the delta area opened his eyes to the material and spiritual needs of the forgotten people who lived there. He received permission from the archbishop to live in the midst of the poor and help them in any way possible. Most of those living in the bayous were French-speaking people, and they were delighted to have a priest who spoke their language and was willing to live among them.

He became so dedicated to his people that every need of theirs was part of his ministry. In his day he served them first of all as their priest. In addition to this vocation, he also served at different times as their father and counselor who was constantly sought out by his parishioners. He was their lawyer, their advocate, their druggist and their teacher.

Actually, Father Girault was pastor of St. Thomas Church in Point-a-la-Hache. From there he took care of about ten mission stations along the river. He traveled to his mission stations in a beat up boat he named "St. Thomas." With his old boat, he was able to maneuver his way in and out of the winding bayous. He carried with him a bell and a gun and he would use both of them to let his parishioners know when he came ashore to see them. As he arrived, he fired the gun in the air, and within a few minutes he would be surrounded by his parishioners, both black and white.

His remarkable work had the enthusiastic support of his superior, Archbishop John Shaw. The archbishop told Mother Katharine that he had bought the boat so that Father Girault might better serve his scattered flock. He also asked that the sisters take a ride on the "St. Thomas" and learn more about the work of the bayou pastor.

Always willing to follow the directions of those in authority, Mother Katharine and Mother Francis Xavier bundled up in their flowing habits and boarded the battered boat for the sail down the Mississippi River. Both of the sisters were a bit apprehensive to say the least, but returned to the dock safe and sound and with a different perspective of what life on the bayous was all about.

They stopped at the tiny, poverty-stricken mission stations along the way. They were delighted as the priest fired his gun at each stop, and within minutes crowds of people were around them eager to talk to their traveling pastor. What the sisters saw in the villages sickened them. Shabby little huts served as part-time schools. Due to the lack of teachers, educational opportunities were usually available only two or three months of the year.

The sisters admired the work of the missionary pastor. They recognized him as a man who had given up the wealth and prestige of a noble family to work among the poorest of God's poor.

Father Girault asked the sisters for help in building a school in the town of City Price. He told them that the children in this village were able to attend a makeshift school for only one month a year. Archbishop Shaw also wrote to Mother Katharine asking for her help in this poorest of villages. She responded with a check to pay for a church at City Price. Quickly the building was constructed. Sunday morning the church was filled with worshipers, and during the week it served as a school for a large number of poor black children. The sisters were delighted with what Father Girault had accomplished with their donation.

Following her boat trip, the mother general decided to visit a few already established missions that had pressing needs. One trip was to the town of New Iberia. This was said to be the home of the banished Acadians, and the place where in a little town cemetery the Evangeline of Longfellow's poem was supposed to be buried. There had been a small church in the town, but the priest begged the sisters to open a small school to take care of his children. On the spot, Mother Katharine assured him he would have a school. She went on to the town of New Roads where a French priest asked her to build "just a very little school." He said that the feeling against any attempt to educate his black children had been intense. His own small school had actually been burned down by a mob of people who wanted no schooling for blacks. In his plea, he told the sisters that in the past year he had allowed black and white people to sit together in his parish church. He felt that the majority of his parishioners were in favor of a new school and they had somehow silenced the hotheads among them. The next year his small school was open to students.

She journeyed then to Mobile, Alabama where ten years before she had given the funds to build St. Peter's Church. Over the years, the community had grown into in a large parish of more than fifteen hundred Catholics—almost evenly divided between black and white. There the pastor happily reported that they had a movie shown in town recently and the black people were allowed to sit in the balcony for the first time. They were not in the best seats, but they actually were there in the same building with the whites. The pastor and mother general recognized this as no small victory.

In the meantime, Monsignor Jeanmard had been named the bishop of Lafayette. It was in his diocese that most of the worst living conditions existed. He was impressed with the facilities in City Price and wrote to the mother general inviting her to come on a tour of the worst areas with him. He reminded the sisters that his diocese had a large number of black Catholics that were being lost to the faith because they had neither churches nor schools in their poor bayous.

In March of 1923, Bishop Jeanmard suggested that the mother general accompany him on a tour of the needy parts of his new diocese. He also wrote to all the priests in his diocese telling them of the work of the Sisters of the Blessed Sacrament, and how much they could help in solving their problems of reaching out to the thousands of blacks who had no contact with the Church.

Mother Katharine was delighted with the invitation to what she called a spiritual excursion in search of souls. She was devastated when she saw the desperate poverty of the rural areas in which so many blacks lived in abject squalor. Hunger and disease were a way of life. There was no opportunity for them to attend Mass and no opportunity for the young people to learn about the Church to which they nominally, at least, belonged. As the bishop and mother general returned from their tour, in tears, she promised that she would do all in her power to bring God to these abandoned communities in Southern Louisiana.

She was true to her word. With a flurry of activity, another Louisiana miracle took place. In a matter of months the new apostolate was in progress. A total of 24 new schools—all simple rural structures—were erected throughout the area. For the most part, the schools ranged in cost from $2,000 to $4,000. They were modest structures containing a few classrooms that were put to great use. The speed with which they were built amazed Bishop Jeanmard and the authorities in the different communities.

As each school opened, most of them filled to capacity. Two graduates from Xavier University were placed in charge of teaching the youngsters. Provision was made for their room and board and each school was supervised by the university. The Drexel Trust Fund paid the salaries of all the teachers, and also paid additional monthly salaries for teachers in public schools where the state provided education to blacks for only a few months a year.

The results of this huge educational undertaking had a profound effect on the poor communities involved. Education was suddenly a possibility to hundreds of young blacks who had never been to school. Scores of families had the opportunity to worship the Lord on a regular basis for the first time in their lives. During the week their children learned about God and their Catholic faith. In the same buildings on Sunday, the whole family could worship the Lord by celebrating the Eucharist together.

In one dramatic construction project, Mother Katharine sought to eliminate the enormous obstacles to the religious education of black boys and girls in the poor, rural areas of the diocese of Lafayette. These obstacles included: extreme poverty, lack of qualified teaching personnel, lack of concern on the part of civil officials and deep-seated racial discrimination against the black community. She spent her whole life trying to counter racial prejudice and was successful in many places, both in the North and the South.

Mother Katharine was a missionary for a good part of her life. It is true that she did not bring the Catholic faith to Louisiana, but she deserves great credit for her efforts to preserve that faith. In those same rural areas of the state in which these schools were built in the mid 1920s, today the faith is flourishing. Those small rural schools have developed into thriving Christian communities—many of them with complete parish plants with church, school, convent and rectory.

The impact of these small Catholic schools cannot be overestimated. They not only preserved the faith for another generation of black believers, but they became the means of encouraging many others who had fallen away to come back to the Church of their parents. Through the years, thousands of young people have come out of these areas to continue their higher education and to take upon themselves responsible positions in their communities. These rural schools, founded through the generous support of Mother Katharine Drexel, have strengthened the faith of those poor black Catholics and given them hope for their future. Much of the credit for this remarkable accomplishment belongs to that bishop and mother general and their spiritual excursion in search of souls.

Mother Katharine's visitation in Lake Charles, Louisiana in 1928.

# CHAPTER 16

# TAR AND FEATHERS TO FOLLOW

The story of Mother Katharine Drexel and the Sisters of the Blessed Sacrament had become a topic of conversation from one end of the country to the other. Newspaper editors were requesting interviews, and the national press was recording the great success of the missionary efforts of the sisters in Louisiana, Virginia, New York, Pennsylvania, New Mexico, Alabama, and other places across the country.

The work of the sisters was applauded throughout the Catholic community. Bishops and church officials here and abroad spoke glowingly of Mother Katharine's work on behalf of the poor and uneducated among the large Native American and black populations. The scores of small Catholic schools, funded by the Drexel Trust Fund and staffed by the Sisters of the Blessed Sacrament, were admired and praised by government officials and educators of all religious faiths. Many of these leaders reached out and sought the help of the sisters in their effort to improve the lot of the nation's poor minority population.

Not everyone, however, approved of what was happening among the disadvantaged blacks and Native Americans. In the 1920s there were still many Americans who thought that public money should not be spent trying to educate them. There were many who believed that there should be separation of the races and that the non-whites had no civil rights. It was a time when the Ku Klux Klan and other white supremacist groups were at the peak of their power.

On several occasions these groups joined together to try to threaten the sisters and their work on behalf of God's poor.

One very dramatic occasion of the demonstration of this latent racial discrimination at its worst occurred in the Spring of 1922. The mother general was making her usual tour of her missionary stations and stopped at a small community she had established the year before in the town of Beaumont, Texas. She realized that since the small church was built, racial tension among the white population had become apparent. Many in the white community objected to having a church in which blacks were allowed to worship freely.

Mother Drexel arrived at the mission to find that Mother Mary of the Visitation, the superior, and the small group of sisters were very disturbed over an incident that had occurred a few days before her arrival. The sisters had arrived as usual for morning Mass only to find a group of parishioners standing before the front door of the church. They were reading from a sheet of paper that was nailed to the door.

When the sisters gathered at the door, they were frightened by the message. In large black letters they read the words, "We want an end to services here. We will not stand idly by, while white priests consort with nigger wenches in the face of our families. Suppress it in one week or flogging and tar and feathers will follow."

When Father Alexis LaPlante, the Josephite priest who served as pastor, arrived for Mass, he read the sign, ripped it off the door and called the disturbed congregation into church for Mass. He told his parishioners that they should not allow such ignorant prejudice to keep them from worshiping in their parish church.

The next morning, as they arrived for Mass, they found another message nailed to the door. It read: "If people continue to come to this church, we will dynamite it."

At this point, the whole town was in turmoil. The police did little to restore calm among the thoroughly frightened members of the parish. The local sheriff came forward and promised he would protect the church and its pastor.

Several members of the Knights of Columbus offered their services to the embattled pastor. One gave Father La Plante a revolver to keep for his protection. For a few days, calm seemed to return. The Mass schedule continued and a few people joined the pastor for the daily Eucharist.

About a week later, a group of violent young men broke into a home not far from the church. They dragged an elderly parishioner of the church from his home and administered a terrible beating. The community was enraged at the brutal beating of the innocent victim of violence.

From that time on, two volunteer members of the Knights of Columbus guarded the rectory each evening. They were convinced that Father La Plante would be the next target for violence. Many of the parishioners were afraid to come to the church for Sunday Mass.

On the day after Mother Katharine arrived for her visitation of the community, the horrible atmosphere dramatically changed.

That afternoon, the Ku Klux Klan held a planning meeting in a meadow near the beleaguered church. They were discussing how they might further intimidate Father La Plante and his frightened parishioners. As the meeting progressed, a huge and violent thunderstorm broke out. As the Klansmen ran for cover, a bolt of lightening struck the leader of the group. As they returned to help, it was clear he was killed instantly.

It was a dramatic solution to the problems of Father La Plante's little Catholic church in Beaumont, Texas. It did not, however, solve the problem of the wholesale denial of the civil rights of minority groups throughout the country.

Mother Katharine left Beaumont very upset about the violent attitude of most of the white people in the community. She was convinced that though the blacks in the South and other parts of the country were free, that freedom did not mean much here, there was so much hatred and violence in the hearts of their neighbors. She vowed to herself that she would spend all her energy so that in her mission schools and churches the civil rights of all people would be respected.

She realized, before many of her contemporary religious, that in 1922 there were really two Americas—whose people were still separated by the color of their skin. The black community she knew wanted to be real American citizens in actual fact as well as according to the law of the land.

She, perhaps more than any other public figure of her day, knew how hard it was for the black members of the community to find a decent place to live, even when they earned enough money to pay for it. She was well aware of the miserable shacks in the rural areas of the South that were called schools. In these tumbled-down shacks, the black students were educated for a few months in the year, if the teacher actually showed up for class.

The incident in Beaumont demonstrated that the white people in the community were not interested in providing a decent education for their black neighbor's children. In fact, they resented black people living in their town and felt no responsibility to provide them with the education every American citizen deserved. They even went out of their way to deny them entrance to all-white schools.

As she reflected on what had happened in that Texas community, Mother Katharine decided that she and her community had to champion the cause of disadvantaged blacks wherever they lived.

Up until this time, the mother general had not given many interviews with the press or accepted many requests to speak at public gatherings. The great success of the work of the Sisters of the Blessed Sacrament resulted in a huge interest in their ministry particularly on the part of the Catholic community. There was a great interest in the life of a millionaire socialite who had given up a life of luxury to work on behalf of poor blacks and Native Americans. She began to realize that in her position, she had an obligation to be a national advocate for those who had no voice.

Her brother-in-law, Walter George Smith, finally convinced her that she should accept more speaking engagements. He told her that her experience, her speaking ability, and her obvious concern for the poor, would help to mobilize the Catholic community to a greater concern for the needs of the disadvantaged minorities in their midst. He was right. She held the attention of large audiences and many times convinced them of their community responsibilities.

They came to listen to her because they knew her name was Drexel, and because she spoke with quiet compassion. Her religious habit and obvious sincerity added credibility.

Sometimes she fearlessly told the audiences things they did not want to hear and truths that they would rather ignore. She caused a bit of disturbance when she told the faculty and students at the University of Notre Dame that there were only two Catholic colleges in Indiana that would accept black students in their classes.

She often spoke of the prejudice of Catholics, especially in the South. She reminded them that there were many Catholics who honestly believed that blacks were somehow inferior to their white brothers and sisters. Many also believed that blacks lacked the intelligence needed to be educated adult members of the community, and that they were good for only manual labor and menial positions.

She told audience after audience that the black community did not want alms from their white neighbors. What the black people wanted was simple justice and the acknowledgement that they were truly full-fledged citizens of the United States of America.

She decided also to attack the large press associations and powerful daily newspaper editors for the way in which they reported news about minority groups. She and her sister, Louise Morrell, attended a meeting of the New York Press Association. They complained to the editors that when a news story was written about some reported crime and the criminal was black, that fact always seemed to end up in the headlines. Faced with the clear evidence, the editors had to admit the complaint was a valid one.

Mother Katharine went on to say: "You do not say, 'White man kills two.' But if it is a black man, his race is always mentioned. This angers good blacks and is obviously unfair because it condemns the whole black community when only a relative few are criminals."

Mrs. Morrell pointed out that most members of the black community are sincerely trying to maintain their reputation and their sense of self-respect. The bad press indicates that most black men live outside the law, while in reality the vast majority are indeed law-abiding citizens who suffer because of all the publicity given to a relatively few criminals.

The editors encouraged them to be vigilant, and when they saw obviously slanted reports of criminal activity to call or write the editor and lodge a complaint. Mother Katharine listened to their advice. She compiled a list of the most powerful newspapers in the country and the names of their editors. In the months ahead many of them received letters from the superior general of the Sisters of the Blessed Sacrament complaining about how they slanted the news and overemphasized the faults of the non-white community. In general, she found this to be an effective means of getting her point across. The end result in many cases seemed to be a more balanced reporting of the local news.

For some time many of her associates and her family and friends had encouraged Mother Katharine to try to get some publicity for her work among the poor. The requests to the Sisters of the Blessed Sacrament for additional religious to take part in their missionary effort required more and more recruits to join their ranks. The need for additional sisters was ever increasing as the work of the congregation spread across the country.

It was a difficult task to let potential postulants know about their important work and how they could help. If the work was to continue to go on, more people had to come to know about their missionary efforts among the poor blacks and native Americans.

By 1928 there were 190 Sisters of the Blessed Sacrament involved in their full-time teaching mission. In addition to the sisters, the congregation also employed about eighty lay teachers who worked in some of the more rural areas. They had grown in a few short years to become one of the largest religious orders in the country. God had blessed their work. Truly the harvest was great.

Many thousands of souls had been touched, but the sisters realized that they had two continuing concerns: the ever-present need for more vocations to the religious life, and the increasing need for additional funds to maintain the schools and churches that depended on the Sisters of the Blessed Sacrament for their financial support.

More and more the superior general had been forced to refuse bishops and priests who came to her seeking additional religious teachers. It was clear to all that it would be necessary somehow to have the general public more aware of what they were trying to accomplish, and then they would be more likely to help.

She sought the advice of Bishop James Corrigan, the rector of the Catholic University of America in Washington. The bishop told her that a good way to spread the news of their work would be to publish their own magazine. She felt that the talent and personnel for this kind of project was just not available to them. But the bishop insisted. The council of the congregation also felt that it was a good idea. To be certain that she had the support and permission of the hierarchy, Mother Katharine consulted her archbishop, Cardinal Dennis Dougherty of Philadelphia. The cardinal was enthusiastic about the project, gave his approval and some substantial support for the new magazine.

Sister Dolores was named the first editor. To raise funds to begin publication, a huge lawn party was held on the grounds of the motherhouse. It was a big success and raised more than $5,000 for the start of the new publication. After months of planning, the first issue of *Mission Fields at Home* came off the presses. It caused an immediate stir.

Of course, the new editor received much unsolicited advice. One fellow editor wrote her to say that she should cut out the complimentary articles about the hierarchy because people would not bother to read them. Even mother general suggested that the magazine could have "a more sparkling, snappy tone."

Most of the responses to the first issue were very positive. *The American Ecclesiastical Review* wished its new competitor *"Ad multos annos."* Father John LaFarge, S.J. of *America* told his readers that the new magazine "showed the simple fact, that it is the doctrine of the Blessed Sacrament which is the magnet that draws blacks to the Church."

Sister Dolores, encouraged by the reaction to her first issue, gathered together her staff and began what was to prove to be a successful effort to spread the word about the work and the needs of the congregation.

During these days the Sisters of the Blessed Sacrament also received help in their second great need—financial support. Over the years, Walter George Smith remained close to his sister-in-law and the work of her congregation. He was a talented lawyer who often gave the sisters important legal advice. He recognized their great financial need necessary to continue their missionary efforts. For some time he was disturbed about the high taxes placed on their income—all of which was used for works of charity. One day he came to the mother general and told her that he had a plan that would greatly reduce the high taxes she was forced to pay.

He spoke to his friend Senator George Pepper who suggested that a special act of Congress might help. He proposed a bill that would free anyone from taxes who gave 90% or more of their income to charitable causes. The bill was immediately criticized for it was thought to be for the benefit of the millionaires and other wealthy business tycoons. Once the word got around that the bill was to benefit the work of Mother Drexel and her sisters, minds were changed. When the politicians and the people came to recognize that her entire fortune was being given to support the desperate needs of the poor members of the black and Native American communities, the criticism ended and the bill passed.

The contributions of Walter George Smith and Senator Pepper were an enormous help in carrying on the charitable work of the congregation. Over the years, it freed up thousands of dollars to help support the missionary efforts of the sisters.

Shortly after he had given this important help on behalf of the work of his sister-in-law, Walter George Smith was stricken and died suddenly. He was buried next to his wife, Elizabeth, in Torresdale. Mother Katharine and her sisters mourned the loss of one who had been a supportive friend of their missionary community for almost fifty years.

# CHAPTER 17

## MORE NEW FOUNDATIONS

As Mother Katharine approached her seventieth birthday, there was no indication of her slowing down her active life. One after another, there were a series of success stories as new missions were established. One of the most remarkable of these was what started as a small and very poor school in the town of Marty, South Dakota. A Benedictine priest, Father Sylvester Eisenmann, served as pastor in this prairie town which was a meeting place for the Yankton Sioux. The tribe flourished during this period in Nebraska and the Dakotas.

In 1922 Father Eisenmann traveled to the motherhouse to plead his case to the sisters. He said that he did not come seeking a financial contribution. He told them that what he desperately needed were teachers, and that if sisters could be found the Lord would provide whatever else was needed.

The priest was so sincere and told such a sad story that the mother general wept when she had to refuse his request. The missionary said he understood and asked that before he left for the Dakotas, he would like to speak to the sisters and describe his work with the Sioux. The sisters were gathered and listened to his story about the small boarding school that he had opened for their children. There were many children who wanted very much to learn, but there were no teachers available to staff his school.

Father Eisenmann finished his talk by asking the sisters a serious question. Trying to avoid the superior's gaze, he asked, "If there are any of you here who could be spared, would you volunteer?"

In response to the question, many sisters raised their hands. After the talk, the missionary made one final plea. He told the mother general that his abbot had told him to get some teachers and the only ones ready were the Sisters of the Blessed Sacrament. He pleaded that she take one more day before she made her final answer. She agreed.

It so happened that Father John Sparrow, from Villanova College, was staying at the motherhouse and came to hear the missionary's talk and the sisters' enthusiastic response. He came to mother asking that she reconsider the request. He even told her that he was going to celebrate morning Mass for that intention. Everyone at Mass the next morning knew what Father Sparrow's intention was.

When the missionary arrived to hear Mother Katharine's reply that afternoon, he was pleasantly surprised. With a smile, the superior told him that in two months' time, three sisters would be at his mission in Marty.

Two months later, true to her word, the sisters arrived at St. Paul's Mission. The mother general accompanied them and had the opportunity to meet Father Sylvester's twenty young children in a small but clean wooden house. He called them his "bronzed angels."

In the tradition of the Benedictine Fathers, it was a simple, poor mission. Right away, Mother Katharine knew that the Lord would truly bless this work. It was difficult country. The winters were extremely cold and snowy. The summers were hot and arid. However, none of the sisters complained and the mission quickly thrived.

Within a matter of months, Father Sylvester had plans for both a high school and an elementary school—all eventually built with material he had salvaged. They were low cost but solid structures and they were filled with eager students.

Mother returned to St. Paul's Mission just two years after bringing her three sisters. She found there were 180 boarding students. In addition to that, there were more than a score of day students as well. They filled every nook and cranny in the buildings. She found that the pastor had hired a new principal and was delighted to find out that she was one of her former students from St. Michael's. It pleased the sisters that one of their own students was now passing on to others what they had learned in one of their schools.

Within five years, the little mission at Marty with only one small frame building had grown into what many people thought was a small prairie town. Suddenly there were small school buildings, houses for school employees, a dairy farm with a creamery, a post office, and eventually the mission's own newspaper—*The Bronze Angel*.

There were many priests and missionaries working among the various tribes. The mission at Marty was special. Its accomplishments were dramatic and became well known through the West. Father Sylvester was a charismatic leader who even found time to serve as the mission's postmaster.

Within a few brief years there were more than four hundred Native American children at St. Paul's Mission. The Sisters of the Blessed Sacrament had provided 23 sisters to teach at the mission. While all this growth was going on, the pastor found time to establish a religious congregation that was called "The Oblates of the Blessed Sacrament." The first novices were young Sioux women.

More than thirty-five years before, the Sisters of Mercy provided a brand new congregation, the Sisters of the Blessed Sacrament, with space in their convent and one of their sisters to serve as Mistress of Novices. Now Mother Katharine was pleased to provide this new religious congregation with space in her convent and a Sister of the Blessed Sacrament to serve as their Mistress of Novices.

Mother Mary of Lourdes was appointed Mistress of Novices of the new congregation. When Mother Katharine discovered that in reality only two Native American girls had made application, she decided to withdraw Mother Mary of Lourdes from the position. But before she was ready to leave Marty, five other ladies were accepted into the congregation. That made a total of seven sisters to start the new congregation. All agreed then that this was a sufficient number for them to formally organize The Oblates of the Blessed Sacrament. The original intention was that only Native American girls were to be admitted, but the ruling was changed to admit any qualified young woman willing to dedicate her life to the missions. In a few short years there were sisters in the new congregation working in missions throughout the large Sioux nation.

As the mother general returned to Cornwells Heights after visiting the mission at Marty, she thanked God for giving Father Sylvester his chance to speak to the sisters and ask his question. The result of that talk was one of the most productive of all missionary efforts among Native Americans, and the Sisters of the Blessed Sacrament were delighted to have played an important part in its success.

The Sisters of the Blessed Sacrament continued to be in great demand. There were requests for the help of the sisters from all across the country. It became increasingly difficult to provide the sisters with the necessary educational training so important for the work of their apostolate. Archbishop Ryan, at the very beginning of the congregation, insisted that each sister be properly prepared for a life of teaching. Over the years the foundress saw to it that every one of her sisters was well prepared before she ever stepped into a classroom to teach.

From the earliest years, the formation of the sisters was a high priority. At the start, those who were to teach in the industrial schools would take the proper courses at Drexel Institute and others attended the University of Pennsylvania and other colleges in the area.

As soon as the Sisters' College was opened at the Catholic University in 1914, Mother Katharine made certain that her teachers attended summer courses. She gave good example by taking courses there on several occasions. Many of her teachers received advanced educational degrees. Doctor Thomas Shields, founder of the Teacher's College in Washington, was a frequent lecturer at the motherhouse. He often spoke to the sisters on child psychology and primary school methods of teaching.

Many distinguished scholars from Villanova, Catholic University, and other colleges and seminaries came to St. Elizabeth's on a regular schedule. To facilitate her sisters, the mother general purchased a house for her teachers on the grounds of the Catholic University. When the demand for teachers continued to grow, she withdrew her sisters from clerical work at the Indian Bureau and sent them to take educational courses to be prepared to teach the hundreds of young people entrusted to the care of the congregation.

It became necessary in 1930, after a period of great demand for their services, that the congregation coordinate all of their educational resources. The mother general decided that she would appoint a Directress of Studies who would be responsible for the teacher training for all of the Sisters of the Blessed Sacrament. The program proved to be a model to be followed by many of the large religious congregations involved in the teaching ministry.

The huge increase in the number of teachers and students in the congregation's educational mission also resulted in the construction of new buildings to satisfy the greater need. The first priority was the building of a separate novitiate so that the novices in the congregation would be allowed to undergo their introduction to the religious life without the distraction of life in the large motherhouse. It also became necessary to construct a much needed annex to the Holy Providence Institute. In addition to all of this, St. Catherine's Hall was erected to house the teacher training program.

The foundress was constantly introducing new ideas and teaching methods to the sisters. She attended many educational conventions and she brought home with her the latest trends in religious education. She wanted to be certain that her black and Native American pupils had the best educational tools available, not like the students of Archbishop Blenk who had to be content with what he called, "the leftovers, if there are any."

In the midst of all of this activity and constant traveling to visit her mission stations, Mother Katharine lived a very penitential life—a life that for the most part she concealed from other members of the community. Our knowledge of this life of prayer and penance comes mostly from the memoirs of her faithful assistant, Mother Mercedes. She served for years as her vicar and the second superior general of the congregation. Mother Mercedes writes of the many times that the foundress would kneel in a space behind the altar with her arms extended in the form of a cross, her eyes riveted on the crucifix above the altar. She would remain fixed in prayer for long periods of time. She always had a deep devotion to the passion and death of the Lord. When Mother Mercedes came upon her in these moments, she seemed as if she were caught up in another world.

Mother Katharine told her assistant that she felt that if she was to spread the Gospel of Jesus to others that she should strive to imitate His way of living. She felt that she should attempt to resemble Him in his physical suffering and to offer Him the reparation of physical pain. She did this quietly without calling attention to herself.

In this period of great expansion when the financial burdens of the mission grew heavy, the foundress sought ways and means of making the new facilities self-supporting. She sought other sources of income or other ways to cut down the enormous expense involved.

With this in mind, she and her companion, Mother Agatha, who was the president of Xavier University, decided to visit St. Mary's Mission in the little community of Omak, Washington. She wrote to the director of the mission, Father Celestine Caldi, S.J. and asked the Jesuit missionary to see if the eighty boys who were boarding at his school could be placed in day schools. If this were possible, then her congregation would be relieved of the great expense of lodging, feeding and clothing the boys. It would result in a large saving of badly needed funds.

The two mothers set out for Washington. It turned out to be a long and difficult journey that would have exhausted women half their age. It took a heavy toll on the two mothers who were both veteran missionaries. They started out from Port Arthur, Texas. Their next stop, after a day and night of travel, was Gallup, New Mexico. They arrived there at two in the morning. After a few hours of sleep, they were on the train again traveling west.

The following night at 10:30 they transferred from the train to a boat that took them to San Francisco where they spent the night with the Sisters of Charity. Early the next morning after the six o'clock Mass, they were on their way to Portland—a 24-hour ride.

They arrived in Oregon at 6:30 a.m. Here they changed cars and set out for Seattle, Washington. They arrived there at 2:30 p.m. and were met by Father Caldi who took them to the convent of the Sisters of St. Joseph. Here they had a couple of hours of rest. At 9:50 p.m. they got on board the train to Wenatchee, which was the nearest station to St. Mary's Mission in Omak.

The mothers arrived at Wenatchee at 1:30 a.m. They were met at the station by a sister who drove them to the mission—a four-hour drive away. They arrived at St. Mary's in time for the six o'clock morning Mass. After the celebration of Mass with all of the sisters and children participating, the exhausted travelers had a few hours rest. At 2:30 in the afternoon, they were up and about again investigating the mission and its facilities.

This six-day trip—by train, boat and car—was typical of the travels of Mother Katharine. She insisted on seeing firsthand all of her many mission stations. It was a grueling schedule but she felt it was her duty as mother general to visit and encourage all of the Sisters of the Blessed Sacrament on a regular basis. The sisters appreciated her dedication and love. Throughout her years as superior, the high morale of the sisters was the envy of other contemporary religious orders.

After looking over the great progress that had been made at St. Mary's, the foundress met with Father Caldi to discuss the future of the school. Up front as always, she asked the pastor about the possibility of having the children attend a day school. The pastor answered by telling the sisters that the nearest day school was six miles away and to get there you had to go over a mountain. To show the sisters what was involved, he took them to the day school. They passed through a forest of high pines and rugged terrain. Quickly they realized that it would be unrealistic to expect the young children to make this daily journey, especially during the winter months.

Undaunted, the mothers suggested they seek the help of the bishop in Spokane. They asked him if he would take over the administration of St. Mary's Mission. The bishop said this would be impossible. The best he could do at the time was to offer the sisters a one-time gift of $2,000. All of them realized that this amount would not go very far in meeting the expenses of room and board for the students and faculty.

Following the unsuccessful efforts to lower costs at the mission, Mother Katharine and her companion were happy to head back to Cornwells Heights and their community. Back at the motherhouse, she gathered the sisters for a friendly chat. She described the long and difficult journey and the disappointing results of their mission. Somehow, she told the congregation, they would find a way to cover their expenses at St. Mary's and continue their important work.

She finished her report by giving her sisters a vision of the future. She wondered what would happen if the people of the United States could come to know the possibilities of these missions in the West. She indicated that in the years to come the purebred red, black and white races would eventually melt away.

As she proved so often throughout her lifetime, Mother Katharine Drexel was far ahead of her time. Who could imagine then that by the first decade of the 21st century the American West would be populated by such a diversity of humanity as exists there today. Over the years, they have come literally from all corners of the earth. From the Orient, the Middle East, Mexico, South America and from Europe as well, they have come to call the American West their new home. Certainly discrimination on the basis of one's race has begun to disappear in our country. Surely Mother Katharine Drexel and her Sisters of the Blessed Sacrament have made a valuable contribution to this acceptance of diversity of race. By their consistent teaching that all men and women, regardless of the color of their skin, share in their common God-given human rights, they sought to provide an education to the disadvantaged of every race. By reaching out to men and women of color, they have helped to sow the seeds of racial harmony in the West and throughout the rest of the country as well.

The sisters at the motherhouse were aware that the long and difficult trip to Washington had taken its toll on their superior. Some members of the council began to encourage her to try to reduce her exhausting schedule of yearly visitation of the mission stations.

# CHAPTER 18

# AT LAST, KATHARINE
# THE CONTEMPLATIVE

For more than three decades, Mother Katharine's life had been a flurry of activity. Her mode of transportation was most often a train. She traveled many months of the year from one end of the country to the other visiting the missions, schools and other institutions operated by the Sisters of the Blessed Sacrament. A series of heart attacks and circulation problems had slowed her down over the years. At 78, her mind remained strong but her body had grown weary. She felt that she was no longer able to provide her beloved sisters with daily guidance and direction and had to give up her annual visitation of the numerous convents, schools and other institutions maintained by her order throughout the country.

It was on one of these frequent visitations that she finally realized it would be impossible to continue at the hectic pace she set for herself for many years. As she planned to leave St. Louis to return to the motherhouse after a series of visitations in the fall of 1935, she decided that she would stop off to visit her sick friend, Sister Stanislaus, who was a patient at St. Vincent's Sanatorium in St.Louis. On the way to the hospital she suddenly felt weak and grew very pale.

Her companion and close associate, Mother Mary of the Visitation, became alarmed and insisted that the driver get them to the hospital as quickly as possible. When they got there Mother Katharine seemed to gain some strength back and said to the sisters, "I'll be all right, just let me sit down for a few minutes."

Despite her protests, the doctor was called to see her. He quickly determined that the elderly nun was far from being all right. After his examination, he discovered that she had a cerebral hemorrhage and that her condition was serious. He prescribed for her a long rest with proper nursing care and suggested that she remain in St. Louis during this period of recuperation. She would have none of that and insisted that they continue home to Philadelphia to her motherhouse. She prevailed on the doctors who only reluctantly agreed to the train trip home.

Mother Mary was so concerned with her condition she insisted that they travel on a train with a drawing room and that Sister Ann, one of the order's most capable and knowledgeable nursing sisters, accompany her in case there were any medical problems on the long journey home.

Before the start of the trip Sister Ann called Mother Mercedes at the motherhouse. She wanted all of the sisters to know that their beloved foundress was in serious condition and that it was of the utmost importance that she should be taken care of immediately. On the second day of the trip to her native city, she had another seizure. Her two companions did their best to make her comfortable. She was visibly weakened and even Mother Katharine herself began to realize that her condition was serious and that she was gravely ill. Her family physician, Doctor Max J. Hermann, met them at the motherhouse and insisted that she be taken immediately to St. Joseph's Hospital to receive a complete physical examination.

The premier cardiologist in Philadelphia, Dr. A.S. Stevens, was called for an immediate consultation. He found extensive arterial blockage and was especially concerned about a serious dilation of the weakened heart. He promptly told the sisters who had gathered at the hospital that her future was clearly in her own hands and that they should encourage her to drastically curtail her activities or face serious consequences.

After talking over the matter with the members of the community present, Dr. Stevens and Sister Ann went to her hospital room to speak with Mother Katharine about the gravity of her condition. The doctor and nurse made it clear that a change of lifestyle would be necessary and that if she cut down on her work and allowed the sisters to handle the details of the order and make the visitations to the communities, she might be able to live for many years. The doctor concluded by telling her, "Mother, you owe it to the community and to humanity to prolong your life."

Mother listened to his words and told him quite clearly that "No one is necessary to do the work of God, Doctor. He could do all the work without any of us becoming involved."

His answer was, "I know that but usually He does not work that way."

She remained a patient at the hospital until the first week of December. She was allowed to return to the motherhouse under the condition that she observe a very strict diet and that she rest free from the stress and responsibilities of overseeing the activities of the vast community she had founded and nourished through the years. With great reluctance she agreed to the regulations imposed upon her by her physicians and her devoted community. All promised to work together to help restore her failing health.

Though confined to a wheelchair, she enjoyed the preparations for the community celebration of the Christmas season. Her celebration was restrained as she faithfully followed the restrictions placed on her activities by her concerned doctors. Her health improved but Doctor Hermann told her plainly that she could no longer keep up her grueling schedule of annual visitations and that probably she would have to curtail her activities to the motherhouse. He told her that if she did not restrict her active lifestyle, there would always be the serious danger of a fatal cerebral hemorrhage.

Her two closest assistants, Sister Mercedes and Sister Agatha, had the task of telling her about this final decision. It proved to be an easier task than they thought it would be. Their leader had spent her entire life trying to accept the will of God. She accepted the verdict of her doctors and her fellow sisters. She realized that her life of frenzied activity and travel would become the life of one who was confined to a wheelchair and that she would rarely be able to leave her beloved mother-house. She had become what she always hoped to be some day—a contemplative religious.

Mother Katharine still had much to offer the community but now it was to be done through her extensive correspondence and her conversations with those who came to visit with her. In this way she continued to influence the spiritual life and progress of the members of her religious order. Everyone was pleased with her recuperation until one day during the Easter season she suddenly slipped from her reading chair and fell to the floor. Once again she was rushed to St. Vincent Hospital.

After a hospital stay of several weeks she came home again to live with her sisters. Weaker and more fragile in appearance she returned requiring the services of a private nurse. The nurse, Miss Super, became her faithful companion who was constantly at her side taking care of all her needs. She was once again able to continue to offer guidance to the community and to begin a new, rewarding life of quiet contemplation.

In 1937, according to the new canon law, her term as superior general came to an end. Mother Katharine wrote to all of the houses of the order declaring that a general chapter would be called with the purpose of electing a new general. In the letter she reminded the sisters that she would soon be 79 years old and she no longer had the health to continue in her office. She told her sisters that "My heart action renders me subject to a condition either of a stroke of paralysis which would incapacitate me or of instant death."

With the support of the foundress, the sisters elected Mother Mercedes as the second superior general and in a reversal of roles named Mother Katharine as her vicar. The sisters gave to their foundress a special place naming her "the first sister" and awarded her many privileges. In this role she continued to serve the Sisters of the Blessed Sacrament with her unique spiritual guidance and outstanding example.

Mother Mercedes served as superior for a short period of three years. She died after suffering months of pain in her cancer ravaged body. At their chapter meeting the sisters elected Mother Mary of the Visitation to be the new superior general and the foundress was relieved of all administrative duties to the order.

The year 1941 marked the 50th anniversary of the founding of the Sisters of the Blessed Sacrament and the religious profession of their foundress. In her modest way Mother Katharine declared that there would be no public celebration of this dual anniversary. The Archbishop of Philadelphia, Cardinal Dennis Dougherty, however, had different ideas. He decreed that there would be a three-day celebration that would involve hundreds of bishops, priests, sisters and laity. One of the highlights of the celebration was a lengthy personal letter of congratulation and commendation from Pope Pius XII. After congratulating her on her golden anniversary, he asked Almighty God "to bless your work in ever more abundant measure, that it may continue to prosper for His greater honor and glory and for the material and spiritual advancement of the more neglected of our beloved American children."

Hundreds participated in the three pontifical Masses and other celebrations. Groups of students came from different parts of the country and from many different schools and institutions conducted by the Sisters of the Blessed Sacrament. It was a colorful cross section of American missions.

When the anniversary celebration was ended there began a series of honorary degrees that were given to the foundress. This included a degree from the Catholic University—the first the university ever offered to a woman. In addition, there were honorary degrees from Duquesne University, St. Joseph College in Philadelphia and Emmanuel College. She accepted these degrees and other tributes and commendations because she did not regard them as meant for herself but rather for all the members of her community.

Because of all the degrees she received, some of her friends began to refer to her jovially as "Doctor Kate." It was at that time that one of the sisters stopped into her room and exclaimed, "Our mother is a doctor." With a smile on her face, she answered her friends with the words, "Oh, I am a lot of doctors now." Through all of the tributes and honors bestowed on her during the golden anniversary celebrations, she remained a humble and modest missionary sister.

The last twenty years of her career she lived a quiet life of prayer and meditation at the Motherhouse in Cornwells Heights, Pennsylvania. Despite a series of heart incidents, her mind remained alert as she continued to plan for the future expansion of her already vast apostolate that benefited the lives of so many of the Lord's disadvantaged children. No longer active in the day-to-day administration of the Sisters of the Blessed Sacrament, she spent almost every waking hour in prayer for her fellow sisters who daily lived the life of missionary workers on behalf of poverty-stricken black and Native Americans.

Very often during those prayer-filled days at the motherhouse, she recalled her early attraction to the religious life. Despite the fact that she lived in a wealthy and influential family, her heart longed for the quiet of the cloister. She assumed the life of an active missionary sister because she was convinced that was the will of God verbalized by the Holy Father himself. Joyfully she lived an active life as a "hands on" superior of a huge missionary order. In the midst of all that activity, it was clear to those who worked with her that she was a woman of intense prayer. Throughout her active years she somehow managed to combine the best features of the contemplative life in a unique way.

As a retired sister, confined to a wheelchair and relieved of all administrative duties, she was able to fulfill her lifelong dream of living the contemplative life in the fullest. She believed that God had decided to give her 96 years of life on this earth so that she would have time to devote the last two decades almost completely absorbed in communion with Him. She made the best of the time that was allotted to her.

Most of the time in the first years of her retirement she spent in chapel in a loft above the sanctuary. She was wheeled there by a sister and she spent many hours praying for her sisters, for their missionary work and for the needs of the Church. She had enthusiastically given all her strength and energy for so many years until the day that her physical strength gave out. There was no job in the order left for her to do except to pray. This she loved to do.

When World War II broke out and her beloved America became involved, her constant prayer was for peace in the world. Each evening she had a period of time that she called her "nocturnal adoration." She would place the life of every soldier in the care of the Sacred Heart. She extended her prayers to all who suffered, to those who were wounded, to those who were victims of bombings on both sides. She prayed that God would forgive all including the Germans, even Hitler himself and even prayed that God would forgive her sins as well.

During these two decades of prayer and penance, Mother Katharine underwent several periods of intense physical suffering. One of her most serious attacks occurred during the

Easter season of 1945. She was rushed to St. Joseph's Hospital where emergency surgery was performed. After an anxious week of intense pain she passed the crisis and regained strength enough to return to the motherhouse.

More and more her condition required that she be confined to her room. When he heard about this, Cardinal Dougherty gave her the privilege of having Mass celebrated in her room. The simple altar that was set up in her bedroom was the wooden altar at which she had received First Holy Communion in the convent of the Religious of the Sacred Heart in Philadelphia. For the rest of her life she joined in the celebration of the Eucharist each day and now more than ever the worship of the Eucharistic Lord became the center of her prayer life and she felt a great peace.

In the fall of that same year she suffered another severe blow. Her "little sister" suffered a heart attack. Mother Philip Neri was sent to San Jose to visit her and report back on her condition. As she returned back to the motherhouse word was received that Louise Morelli had died. When Mother Katharine was told the news she began to cry great sobs. Up until this time no one had seen her weep. "I must stop this," she said over and over. "It is not that I want anything different from what God wants but I cannot believe that life is taken from me —I cannot."

Louise had been sister and life-long companion. Her passing was a crushing blow and she was deeply moved by the loss.

As the years went on her memory began to fail and she lost a lot of weight and became very frail. For the last five years in life she was confined to her bed. In 1953 she received her last award as "Philadelphia's Most Distinguished Lady." She hardly knew the award had been given her. She had left the material world and spent most of her waking hours in the world of the spirit.

During the day she prayed almost all of the time. This became her daily task. She was still working for the Lord as she had worked all her life. The work of her hands and the long trips of visitation were no longer possible. Now she spent her time storming heaven with prayers for all those she loved especially her sisters and the black and Native American children still in her spiritual care.

Her 96th and last year of life was a time of great grace for her. Her foundations throughout the country flourished and grew in numbers. New convents were built and the number of disadvantaged children being taken care of by the order reached a new high. The members of her community were convinced that their continued great success was the result of her devout prayer life and her example of holiness. During her last months of life the sister who attended her throughout the night was in awe of the few hours spent at sleep and the many sleepless hours of communion with the Lord. To the very end, she was a shining example for all who considered her in a special way to be their mother. Through her letters, diaries and other writings she continued to offer her sisters guidelines for living the life of a missionary religious.

# CHAPTER 19

## THE HOMECOMING

Mother Katharine celebrated her ninety-sixth birthday quietly on November 26, 1954. She sat up in the huge chair that had been her father's favorite chair in the library of their home on Walnut Street. She was feeble and frail. On the insistence of the sisters caring for her, she opened some cards and presents. The next month, Christmas found her even weaker. She was barely aware of what was going on around her and took little notice of the numerous gifts she received from her many friends and admirers.

On the January day that she celebrated the anniversary of her solemn profession, she seemed to brighten up. She sat up in her chair and looked over the cards and gifts that she had received. She talked to the new superior, Mother Anselm, and her nurse, Sister Clement. She talked about her little sister Louise and wrapped her white shawl around her and told the sisters that this was her sister's last gift before she died.

Early in February, she had a definite bad spell and on the 20th her new physician, Doctor John McFadden, was called in and diagnosed her condition as lobar pneumonia. All were concerned that because of her advanced age, this attack of pneumonia might prove to be fatal. To the surprise of the doctor, she began to improve and in a few days he announced that she had recovered from the bout with pneumonia. He did indicate that a very definite heart murmur was still clearly evident.

On the night of March 2, just after the community celebrated Benediction of the Blessed Sacrament, Sister Clement rushed into the chapel to find Mother Anselm, the new Superior. She reported that the foundress seemed to be strangling from a very severe coughing spell. By the time that the two sisters got back to her room, the patient had recovered from the spell. Sister Clement discovered that her respiration was very rapid. The Bucks County Rescue Squad was called and quickly an oxygen tent was installed.

Through all of the commotion, Mother Katharine calmly watched the installation of the tent and the sister-nurse recalls that she smiled sweetly at the attendants as they finished with their work.

Doctor McFadden arrived and examined the patient who seemed to be breathing better. All stood vigil at the bedside as the hours quietly passed. About 4 a.m. everything seemed fine and the doctor instructed that the oxygen tent be removed.

After the doctor left, the foundress continued to improve. To everyone's amazement at 8 o'clock she ate her usual good breakfast and the doctor was informed that she was much better.

About a half hour later, suddenly her respiration became very rapid. This time the oxygen did not relieve the breathing problem. It was clear now that the patient was dying. The priest and doctor were quickly called back. Having received the last rites from the convent chaplain, Father John Nugent, she died about 9:05 a.m. surrounded by her sisters kneeling at prayer.

All were impressed with the serenity of her passing. Her long years of prayer and her frequent meditations on death prepared her for her last moments. Those at her bedside reported that she suddenly opened her eyes looking straight ahead, then closed them again, gave a sigh and breathed her last.

During her last years she had repeatedly said that she prayed for two things: to spend some time in prayerful contemplation and that she be allowed somehow to work to the end. The Lord she so faithfully served allowed both her dying wishes to come true. Her long years of service combined in a unique way the best of both the active and contemplative religious life.

As soon as he heard word of her death, Archbishop John O'Hara offered the sisters the Philadelphia cathedral for the funeral Mass. Mother Anselm was in charge of arrangements. She decided to bring home to the motherhouse sixty of the older sisters who had worked with the foundress in her active days. She decided that Mother Katharine's body would be brought to the motherhouse to lie in state for two days so that her many friends in Philadelphia could attend the wake.

Throughout Sunday morning, the sisters of the motherhouse community and those who had already gathered from neighboring missions knelt in the chapel continuously reciting the rosary while four other sisters stood as an honor guard around the casket. Later in the morning, Mother Anselm provided some private time for the members of the Sisters of the Blessed Sacrament, time for prayerful remembrance of her long and devoted life, and time for her grief-stricken daughters to say their last good-bye together. The community finished by thanking God for her long and productive life and asking Him to continue to bless the congregation that she loved and served.

Once the community had the opportunity to mourn together on the loss of their beloved mother, they opened the doors of the motherhouse so that the world might have an opportunity to share their grief. What happened amazed the sisters of the community and everybody else. People from every walk of life came to mourn the loss of one whom they considered to be their mother in a real way. They came from all directions and from long distances and around the corner in Cornwells Heights. Each had his or her story about how Mother Katharine Drexel had changed their life.

They came in a steady stream, despite the cold, the wind and the heavy rain. The streets for miles around were clogged with traffic. It became necessary to assign a group of police to assist in the control of traffic in the area.

The miserable weather seemed to have no effect on the huge crowds. They came by the hundreds to pass in single file around the casket. The elderly moving along with the help of canes, little children clinging to their parents' hands, teenage boys and girls walking by with unaccustomed reverence. Slowly they continued in what seemed to be an unending line.

The sisters allowed their mourning visitors to touch the casket. The four sisters in the honor guard took religious articles from them and reverently touched them to the body. Some broke the silence by telling those around them the reason they were there. One of her former students in Rock Castle, after a silent prayer, said to those around him that "We came to look upon a saint. She surely was a saint to live the way she did."

Many parents brought their small children to what must have been their first wake. One of the sisters told of a man who held up his young child so that he could see the body of Mother Katharine and told him, "Take a good look at that nun, my son. Someday you can say that you looked upon a saint."

The crowds continued all afternoon into the evening. As Mother Anselm watched the long lines of rain-drenched mourners, she promised that all who came would have the opportunity to view the body. As a result it was just after midnight before the chapel doors were closed after the last visitor.

The next morning, early Mass was celebrated for the repose of her soul. The chapel was filled with people who came from all over. One large group of Holy Providence School graduates left Washington at midnight so that they might arrive in time for Mass. Included in the congregation were all of the sisters who had returned to Philadelphia and many parishioners from nearby parishes.

Following the Mass on Monday morning, the chapel doors were open again to receive the throngs that waited outside. As they had the day before, a long line of mourners solemnly walked by the coffin to pay their respects. Helen Grace Smith, her life-long friend with whom she grew up in Torresdale, stood by the coffin and spoke of the foundress in these words: "Her love of personal poverty made her oblivious to comfort of any kind. She went long distances, in all kinds of conveyances, and often walking when there was no other way, and she went simple, silent and unknown."

In the cold, wintery night, they gathered outside in small groups talking about the dedicated missionary sister whom most considered to be a saint. Finally the exhausted sisters closed the chapel doors to prepare the coffin for the early morning trip to the cathedral in Philadelphia.

Early on Tuesday morning, several priests celebrated Mass in the motherhouse chapel. Promptly at 7:30 a.m. the casket was closed and the sisters began to take their place in the funeral cortege. Among those who took part in the funeral procession were Mother Irenaeus, the Sister of Mercy who had been with the foundress in Pittsburgh sixty years earlier, members of the Indian Sister Oblates from South Dakota and the Black Sister Oblates from Baltimore.

A police escort led the funeral procession as the foundress left her beloved motherhouse for the last time. The citizens of her native city gathered in groups along the streets to watch the funeral procession make its way downtown. When the hearse arrived at the doors of the Cathedral, the church was already filled to overflowing. Despite the bitter temperatures and cold wind many stood outside to catch a glimpse of the coffin as it entered and left the church.

As the casket moved down the main aisle, the senior members of the Sisters of the Blessed Sacrament followed the body of their beloved mother and took the front places reserved for them. As the celebrant and assisting clergy reached the sanctuary, the choir from St. Charles Seminary in Overbrook intoned the *Introit* of the funeral Mass, *"Requiem Aeternam, Dona eis, Domine."*

The Most Reverend Gerald O'Hara, the archbishop of Philadelphia, celebrated the Mass. Newspapers reported that more than 250 clergy participated in the funeral Mass. Included were: two archbishops, six bishops, two abbots and provincials and major superiors from more than a dozen religious orders. Unable to find seats in the sanctuary, the attending priests overflowed into the front pews of the enormous church. It was a worthy tribute to the woman who gave more than nine decades of service to the Church and her most disadvantaged members.

Bishop Joseph McShea preached the funeral sermon. He spoke of the work of Mother Katharine on behalf of the neglected children of poor black and Native American families. He said in part: "She was activated, inspired and impelled by an insatiable love of God. Hers was not a humanitarianism that stops where true love should begin. She was not a mere social reformer, educator, or philanthropist striving to better the condition of her fellow man while permitting him to ignore God. She was a true missionary with a contemplative heart."

Just before the final absolution of the funeral liturgy, Archbishop O'Hara came over to the pews occupied by Mother Katharine's daughters, the Sisters of the Blessed Sacrament. On behalf of the archdiocese and her friends throughout the country, he offered the sisters the sympathy of all who loved her. Speaking on behalf of the sisters, Mother Anselm thanked the archbishop for offering the cathedral for the funeral ceremony. In reply, he said to her, "You see mother, even this huge church is not large enough for this funeral."

Following the final absolution, the procession of bishops, priests and sisters formed again and followed after the mortal remains of the Reverend Mother Katharine Drexel as the coffin made its way down the long main aisle. As a fitting tribute to her life and work, the coffin was carried by six men—two white men who worked for years at the motherhouse, two black men from the South and two Indians from the Southwest.

As they carried the casket through the wide doors of the cathedral church, it passed the familiar statue of Our Lady of the Benediction, holding in her arms the Child Jesus. The statue was the gift of Francis Drexel. Often he and his young daughter Kate would pass before the familiar image of Jesus and his Mother as they left church after Sunday Mass. This was the last time his daughter would pass that statue as her body was carried through the cathedral doors.

As the long funeral procession made its way through the streets of the city and neared the motherhouse, it took a detour at Torresdale in order to pass slowly by Eden Hall. At the main entrance, the Religious of the Sacred Heart stood with lighted candles in their hands. As the hearse passed by, their students joined them as they sang *"In Paradisum."* Meanwhile the teachers and students standing in front of the nearby St. Catherine of Siena School recited the rosary.

The procession made its way to the motherhouse. In front of St. Elizabeth's Convent a group of neighbors gathered in the cold to say their last farewell to their beloved friend. Through the foresight and concern of Mother Mary of the Visitation many years before, a burial crypt had been set in place underneath the motherhouse chapel. This is where the sisters wanted her remains to rest. As the coffin was interred in the crypt, Father John Nugent, motherhouse chaplain, gave the final blessing. Over the years many thousands of the faithful have made the pilgrimage to this small shrine in Cornwells Heights to honor the memory of the foundress of the Sisters of the Blessed Sacrament.

During the next few days, messages of sympathy poured into the motherhouse. Pope Pius XII wired his personal message of condolence on the death of this special daughter of the Church. He was joined by hundreds of expressions of sympathy from cardinals, bishops, public officials, sisters, priests, former students and the public at large. In the weeks that followed, countless religious congregations and missionary groups from all parts of the world sent expressions of their heartfelt sense of loss.

Many of the expressions of sympathy to the motherhouse indicated that there were thousands of the faithful across America—especially among the Native American and black communities —who believed that she was a saint. They openly spoke of not praying for her but to her. All seemed convinced that some day soon the Church would confirm their belief by the rite of canonization.

Scores of newspapers throughout the country praised her life of dedicated service to the disadvantaged. *The New York Times* said that "She gave her millions as cheerfully as she devoted her life." The Catholic press was unanimous in their editorial praise for her work on behalf of the neglected.

It seemed appropriate that the words of her hometown newspaper the *Catholic Standard and Times* would best summarize the impact of her great legacy. They closed their lead editorial with these very appropriate words:

"One of the most remarkable women in the history of America was called home to God yesterday.

The priests and people of the Archdiocese of Philadelphia have been proud to claim her as their own, and yet she belonged so truly to all America, but especially to the poor and forgotten people of America—our Indians and Negroes. Reverend Mother Katharine Drexel belonged to Philadelphia and to America, but one cannot help seeing in the story of her life that she belonged to God."

# CHAPTER 20

# THE MAKING OF A SAINT

Cardinal John Krol, the archbishop of Philadelphia, began in 1964 the thirty-six year process that ended with the canonization of St. Katharine Drexel on October 1, 2000. Patiently, all these years, the Sisters of the Blessed Sacrament waited as the lengthy process of the making of a saint took its course. Most of those still waiting—and in the United States of America there are 28 potential saints who are still waiting—may have to wait decades, or even a century, before they are canonized as saints by the Catholic Church.

The path to sainthood has been described by observers as the world's most complex, drawn out legal process. In many ways it puts a large-scale legal class action suit to shame. In most cases it requires years of hard work and endless research. Those who participate are often called upon to have the patience of Job for a task that goes on and on.

Sister Ruth Catherine Spain served for years as one of the chief promoters of sainthood for the foundress of the Sisters of The Blessed Sacrament. At present, she serves as the director of the St. Katharine Drexel Guild in Bensalem, Pennsylvania. During the long years required for the completion of the canonization process, she and guild members throughout the country worked tirelessly in an enormous effort to promote the cause through the various steps of the complicated process. Much of the time of guild members was given over to prayer as they literally stormed heaven on behalf of their candidate for sainthood.

Prayer played an important part in their success. The hard work of research and a good public relations effort aided the cause. Members of the guild will readily admit that success required divine intervention. Pope John Paul II decided that Mother Katharine should be canonized a saint after two extraordinary events were recognized as miraculous by the Church. The proof of these miraculous divine interventions was necessary to complete the long and difficult process.

On Sunday, October 1, 2000, Pope John Paul II formally canonized Mother Katharine as a saint of the Roman Catholic Church. To understand how this came about, it is necessary to know something about the canonization process. In their website, the Sisters of the Blessed Sacrament explained the canonization process in this way.

Following the formal introduction of the cause in 1964, there were three major stages in the process.

1. SERVANT OF GOD (Venerable Katharine) This stage requires the proof that the candidate lived a life of faith and morals.

2. BEATIFICATION (Blessed Katharine) This stage requires an extraordinary posthumous event that is recognized as miraculous by the Church. By that we mean an event that cannot be explained according to the laws of human science and is attributed to divine intervention through the mediation of the Servant of God who has been invoked by the faithful.

3. CANONIZATION (St. Katharine) This stage requires a second extraordinary event after beatification that is recognized as miraculous by the Church.

There are several successive steps that lead up to the beatification ceremony. At the beginning of the process the postulator of the cause must gather all of the evidence—whatever historical and clinical documentation is available. Then the witnesses must be brought together and deposed. Then there is a critical study of all the evidence and the writing of "the *Positio*"— a legal brief that seeks to prove the extraordinary nature of the event.

In the case when the event is a physical occurrence, it must be examined by a medical board of specialists. After the medical group has approved its authenticity, then there has to be an assessment by a special board of appropriate theologians. Following this approval, the *Posito* is brought before the 25 cardinals and bishops who are members of the Congregation for the Causes of Saints. Only after the approval of all these boards and congregations is the matter turned over to the judgment of the Holy Father. Only after the entire process is completed, can the Holy Father beatify the Servant of God.

In order for the candidate who has been beatified to be canonized, a second extraordinary event must be recognized. This new miracle must have occurred after the beatification process. The event must go through the same process as the first extraordinary event, and must be approved by the same boards and congregations. Only after all of this is completed can the Holy Father canonize the candidate as a saint.

Most Catholics have no idea about the long and difficult road that must be followed. Once the Vatican has declared there are no objections to moving forward and bestows the title "Servant of God" upon the candidate, then the research really begins. Every nook and cranny of the person's life must be examined in excruciating detail.

In the case of Mother Katharine Drexel, there are mountains of documents in the archives of the Sisters of the Blessed Sacrament in the motherhouse at Cornwells Heights. She wrote diaries, journals and hundreds of letters that date back to her earliest days. The director of the Archives, Stephanie Morris, Ph.D., and her staff handled the hundreds of inquiries involved in the canonization process. All of the available material and the well organized "Annals of the Sisters of the Blessed Sacrament 1899-1955" made it possible for the process to move more quickly than other causes for canonization that sometimes have long years of delay.

The first of the two accepted miracles occurred in 1974. The Philadelphia-area doctors had given up hope and a bone-dissolving infection had rendered the 14 year-old Robert Gutherman deaf in his right ear. His mother was resigned to the permanent loss of the boy's hearing. What she prayed for was the end to his terrible pain and suffering. She reported that the pain caused by the infection was so great that Robert was forced to sleep with his head on a hot-water bottle to dull the ache.

His mother called the Sisters of the Blessed Sacrament at their motherhouse in Cornwells Heights, and sought their help. The convent was near the Gutherman's home in Bensalem. The sisters urged the family to pray to Mother Drexel. They explained that she would intercede in Robert's behalf and ease his great pain.

One night, scared and all alone in his hospital bed, Robert prayed to Mother Katharine. As a youngster he had served Mass at the convent chapel. When he awoke in the morning, the pain was gone and his hearing was restored to normal.

Robert recalls that when the doctor examined his ear he said, "I can't believe what I am seeing. His body is healing itself." In his records after the examination, the doctor wrote, "Is this possible?"

In 1988, after years of investigation that included testimony of physicians, analysis of X-rays, and the approval of the Congregation for the Causes of Saints, the Church judged Robert's healing to be miraculous. As a result, Mother Katharine was beatified.

Amanda "Amy" Wall of Bensalem was born with nerve deafness in 1992. This condition was confirmed by a battery of medical tests in September of 1993. In November, Constance Wall, the child's mother, heard about the miraculous restoration of hearing to Robert Gutherman's right ear. The family got together with friends in the neighborhood to pray to Blessed Katharine. They went to the motherhouse of the Sisters of the Blessed Sacrament and borrowed a relic of the beatified mother general and touched it to the child's ears.

The prayers continued. A few days later, an alert teacher in the pre-school that Amy attended, recognized a change in the child's responses to questions. Hearing tests were given and the child was found to have normal hearing in both ears.

One of the promoters of the cause of canonization, Reverend Paolo Monlinari, S.J., announced that Amy had been born with a neuro-sensory hearing loss. He added that no scientific explanation had been found for Amy suddenly being able to hear when she had never heard before.

The extraordinary event was referred to Rome. There it went through the same process as the previous miracle. After the evidence was gathered together and disposition of witnesses was accomplished, a position paper (*Positio*) was written to prove the extraordinary nature of the event. After an approval from a board of theologians and the members of the Congregation for the Causes of Canonization, the Holy Father decreed that this was indeed a miraculous event. Pope John Paul II announced that the Foundress of the Sisters of the Blessed Sacrament would be canonized a saint of the Roman Catholic Church at 10 a.m. on October 1, 2000 in St. Peter's Square in Rome.

When she heard the news, Mrs. Wall fought back tears and hugged her child. She was quoted by the Associated Press as saying, "We are so thrilled. We thank Blessed Katharine for her intercession for our daughter and we thank Almighty God for the blessing of this wonderful miracle. What a wonderful day."

A reporter asked Mrs. Wall just how clear Amy's hearing had become. She laughed and said that "She can hear somebody say 'cookie' from a mile away."

In the early morning hours on October 1, thousands of the faithful made their way to St. Peter's Square for the ceremonies marking the canonization of Mother Katharine Drexel. Two other religious sisters and 120 martyrs were also named as saints of the Roman Catholic Church on this same day. The program began with almost an hour of prayers and songs in four different languages. During this time the congregation continued to grow as thousands passed through metal detectors set up around the perimeter of the huge plaza. The rain came down in torrents while thunder rumbled overhead. The plaza was set up with areas of seats for the followers of the soon-to-be named saints. Each group was identified by distinctive scarves and each was assigned a certain area in which to sit. The torrent of rain caused many of the pilgrims to rush to the nearest seat. Instead of each group sitting together, the result was that all four groups—Americans, Chinese, Africans and Spaniards—were all seated mixed in together. Viewing the scene, one of the sisters from Philadelphia remarked that Mother Katharine would be pleased with the arrangement—all of the races and nationalities sitting together as one family. At precisely 10 a.m., the huge central doors of the Basilica burst open and the solemn canonization Mass began with a long procession of bishops, cardinals and other church dignitaries, followed by Pope John Paul II.

The highlight of the service came at 10:30 when the pope solemnly declared that Mother Katharine Drexel was a "Sancta Catholica." She was now to be formally known as "St. Katharine Drexel." It seemed at this precise moment—10:32 a.m.—the torrential rain that drenched the plaza since early morning came to a halt and the sun began to push the clouds aside. Suddenly a sea of umbrellas disappeared as the huge congregation welcomed the Roman sunshine. The sunny interlude did not last long but for at least a half hour, the congregation could take part in the colorful ceremonies without ducking under an umbrella.

In his homily, Pope John Paul put the life of the new saint in perspective. He spoke of her sacrificial living in these words:

"Mother Katharine Drexel was born into wealth in Philadelphia. But from her parents she learned that her family possessions were not for them alone but were meant to be shared with the less fortunate."

"Later, she understood that more was needed. With

great courage and confidence in God's grace, she chose to give not just her fortune but her whole life totally to the Lord. May her example help young people in particular to appreciate that no greater treasure can be found in this world than in following Christ with an undivided heart and in using generously the gifts we have received for the service of others and for the building of a more just and peaceful world."

The rain began again and intensified. Huddled under umbrellas the 1,500 people from the Archdiocese of Philadelphia, and hundreds more from across the country, joined in the celebration of the Eucharist honoring St. Katharine Drexel. Their archbishop, Cardinal Anthony Bevilacqua, summed up their feelings on this special day when he said, "Now Katharine Drexel is a saint not only for the small community of Philadelphia but for the whole world. She is a great model for all people—no matter what color or race—and for those with resources. She gave completely of her great resources."

As the 100,000 rain-soaked members of the congregation made their way out of a soggy St. Peter's Square on that Sunday afternoon, Sister Ruth Catherine Spain, S.B.S. looked over the scene. She had spent the last five years of her life on behalf of the Sisters of the Blessed Sacrament promoting the cause for canonization for their foundress. With a contented sigh and a smile on her face, she turned to her companions and said, "I can hardly believe it. The day's finally come."

The next day most of the pilgrims from Philadelphia, New Orleans and the Southwest missions came back to St.Peter's Square. The pope came back and so did the rain. It was a special papal audience for those who had come to Rome to celebrate the canonization ceremonies on Sunday. Once again, there were the claps of thunder and the torrents of rain.

The pilgrims sat on plastic chairs. At the appointed hour, Pope John Paul, standing in his shiny, bright, jeep-like popemobile, was driven through the square. From his open car, he blessed the throngs, once again huddled under umbrellas. The Holy Father, standing in front of the canopy-covered altar, spoke of the virtues of the newly canonized saint. He spoke to the Americans in English and closed with these words, "Mother Drexel placed her confidence in the Lord and gave her life and wealth totally to his service. Her apostolate bore fruit in the establishment of many schools for Native Americans and blacks, and served to raise awareness of the continuing need, even in our own day, to fight racism in all its manifestations." As the brief service came to an end, the important guests lined up to meet the Holy Father and receive his blessing. As the dignitaries waited to greet the pope, the assembled congregation, sitting in the rain, grew restless. As the president of Xavier University, Dr. Norman Francis, was introduced to John Paul II, the huge special audience gathered in St. Peter's Square, suddenly sounded much like a crowd at the Louisiana Superdome.

From the American delegation, just in front of the outdoor altar, a chant with a distinctive New Orleans flavor broke out as the crowd began to sing, "Oh, when the saints, go marchin' in! Oh, when the saints go marchin' in! Lord, I want to be in that number, when St. Katharine goes marchin in!"

The pope and other Vatican officials seemed puzzled as the rain-soaked audience stood and joined in the singing. Gregorian chant it was not. But it was easy to imagine, from her place in heaven, St. Katharine Drexel, surrounded by the black and Native American youngsters she brought with her, smiling down on her soggy but happy children.

As the impromptu concert ended, a reporter asked one of the Navajos who had come from Arizona for the canonization, why Mother Drexel had become a saint. His reply was simple but said it all. He answered, "When nobody else did, she loved us."

Amen.

# BIBLIOGRAPHY

Aumann, Jordan, O.P. *Saints of the Roman Calendar.* New York: Alba House, 1992.

Burton, Katharine. *The Golden Door.* New York: P.J. Kennedy & Sons, 1957.

Duffy, Sister Consuela, S.B.S. *Katharine Drexel: A Biography.* Bensalem, PA: Mother Katharine Drexel Guild, 1966.

Garraty, Jim, ed. *Encyclopedia of American Biography.*

LaFarge, Reverend John, S.J. *The Catholic Viewpoint on Race Relations.* Garden City, NY: Hanover House, 1956.

Letterhouse, Sister M. Dolores, S.B.S. *The Francis A. Drexel Family.*Privately printed, Camden, NJ, 1939.

McDonald, Rev. William J., D.D. ed. *New Catholic Encyclopedia.* New York: McGraw-Hill Books, 1966.

McHenry, Robert, ed. *Liberty's Women.* Springfield, MA: G. and C. Merriam Co., 1980.

Morris, Stephanie, Ph.D. Archivist. *Annals of the Sisters of the Blessed Sacrament.* 1893-1955.

Rahill, Peter. *The Catholic Indian Missions.* Washington, D.C.: Catholic University of America, 1953.

*Sisters of the Blessed Sacrament Golden Jubilee 1891-1941.*
Bensalem ,PA .

Spain, Sister M. Ruth Catherine, S.B.S. *Mother Katharine Drexel Guild.*

Yost, Reverend Charles E., S.C.J. *In His Likeness.* Pinellas Park, FL: Priests of the Sacred Heart of Jesus, 1988.

# Additional Titles Published by Resurrection Press, a Catholic Book Publishing Imprint

| | | |
|---|---|---|
| A Rachel Rosary | *Larry Kupferman* | $4.50 |
| Blessings All Around | *Dolores Leckey* | $8.95 |
| Catholic Is Wonderful | *Mitch Finley* | $4.95 |
| Come, Celebrate Jesus! | *Francis X. Gaeta* | $4.95 |
| Days of Intense Emotion | *Keeler/Moses* | $12.95 |
| From Holy Hour to Happy Hour | *Francis X. Gaeta* | $7.95 |
| Grace Notes | *Lorraine Murray* | $9.95 |
| Healing through the Mass | *Robert DeGrandis, SSJ* | $9.95 |
| The Healing Rosary | *Mike D.* | $5.95 |
| Healing Your Grief | *Ruthann Williams, OP* | $7.95 |
| Heart Peace | *Adolfo Quezada* | $9.95 |
| Life, Love and Laughter | *Jim Vlaun* | $7.95 |
| Living Each Day by the Power of Faith | *Barbara Ryan* | $8.95 |
| The Joy of Being an Altar Server | *Joseph Champlin* | $5.95 |
| The Joy of Being a Catechist | *Gloria Durka* | $4.95 |
| The Joy of Being a Eucharistic Minister | *Mitch Finley* | $5.95 |
| The Joy of Being a Lector | *Mitch Finley* | $5.95 |
| The Joy of Marriage Preparation | *McDonough/Marinelli* | $5.95 |
| The Joy of Music Ministry | *J.M. Talbot* | $6.95 |
| The Joy of Preaching | *Rod Damico* | $6.95 |
| The Joy of Being an Usher | *Gretchen Hailer, RSHM* | $5.95 |
| Lights in the Darkness | *Ave Clark, O.P.* | $8.95 |
| Loving Yourself for God's Sake | *Adolfo Quezada* | $5.95 |
| Mother Teresa | *Eugene Palumbo, S.D.B.* | $5.95 |
| Our Grounds for Hope | *Fulton J. Sheen* | $7.95 |
| Personally Speaking | *Jim Lisante* | $8.95 |
| Practicing the Prayer of Presence | *Muto/van Kaam* | $8.95 |
| Prayers from a Seasoned Heart | *Joanne Decker* | $8.95 |
| Praying the Lord's Prayer with Mary | *Muto/vanKaam* | $8.95 |
| 5-Minute Miracles | *Linda Schubert* | $4.95 |
| Season of New Beginnings | *Mitch Finley* | $4.95 |
| Season of Promises | *Mitch Finley* | $4.95 |
| Soup Pot | *Ethel Pochocki* | $8.95 |
| Stay with Us | *John Mullin, SJ* | $3.95 |
| Surprising Mary | *Mitch Finley* | $7.95 |
| Teaching as Eucharist | *Joanmarie Smith* | $5.95 |
| What He Did for Love | *Francis X. Gaeta* | $5.95 |
| Womansoul | *Pat Duffy, OP* | $7.95 |

For a free catalog call 1-800-892-6657